Warning: This book contains graphic descriptions of rape and violence. There is also reference to homophobia.

PRAISE FOR *THE FIX*

'Fans of *Law and Order SVU* will love this'
Louise Mullins

Long-listed for the Lucy Cavendish Fiction Prize 2020

DARK EDGE PRESS

THE FIX

M. A. RUSSO

Published in 2021 by Dark Edge Press.

Y Bwthyn
Caerleon road,
Newport,
Wales.

www.darkedgepress.co.uk

Text copyright © 2021 M. A. Russo

Cover Design: Jamie Curtis

Cover Photography: M. A. Russo/Canva

A CIP catalogue record for this book is available from the British Library.

ISBN (eBook): B09CZHDJ7L
ISBN (Paperback): 979-8-7507-0350-0

CONTENTS

PROLOGUE

You'd been going to the old store cupboard at the back of the gym hall every day for the past week, smugly confident the bullies were too stupid to even notice the cupboard door, let alone think that you were lurking somewhere inside. You'd rearranged the old vault horse and benches to make a wall to sit behind - in among the dusty dumbbells and rotting, leathery footballs – just in case any of the losers opened the door and looked in. So far, that hadn't happened. You found this place in desperation; sick of coming out of school and enduring the name-calling, the spitting, the prodding, stealing your books, even pissing on you at the stinking, school urinals. It was becoming worse and God knows what the stupid, thick morons were going to do to you next.

You liked going home after everyone else. The streets were quieter. Normally, you'd stay in your hideout for ten minutes then cautiously emerge, making sure no one was around and the door was closed tightly behind you, but today was different. Today was Thursday. On Thursdays the senior girls had netball training after school. You knew this because last Thursday you got so caught up reading your book, Hawking's *A Brief History of Time*, that ironically you lost all track of time. The girls' echoing laughter and shrieks in the shower room, accompanied by perfumed wafts of rose and lavender soap, drew both your eye and your nose to the crack in the cement between the bricks. It was strange you hadn't noticed the crack before, but it was just above your head when sitting, which meant you had to kneel to peer through the draughty hole. But then you saw them. Naked and wet, the girls cavorted around, throwing soapy sponges and squirting shampoo at each other. Their wet breasts shimmered and jiggled as they moved. They seemed so oblivious to the fact they were naked, comfortable in their own skins. You gasped and pulled back. You hadn't expected to see nude, wet, senior girls with breasts, and hair down there. Your hand reached down to your crotch, where your trousers felt tight over your hardness. You'd never felt that before. It felt good. You were confused. It was getting late and your mother would be worried. Reluctantly, you had to go home.

Last week you told your mother you lost track of time, reading in the library. Your mother didn't like lies, but it was only a half lie, so you didn't feel too bad. God knows when children lie, and that wasn't good. You thought all week about those naked girls in the shower room. You wanted more, to see more. Your excitement bubbled in anticipation as you looked forward to today. You even mentally thanked the idiot bullies for helping you find your sanctuary and this visual prize. So there you were, in your lair. You had told your mother that you would be late home because you would go to the library to get a new book. Another lie. Would God punish you?

Your breathing was heavy, your palms

sweating and your knees uncomfortable against the uneven parquet floor, but that wasn't going to distract your focus, not today. You sat patiently waiting for any sounds that the girls had finished their game and were heading to the showers, but none came. Maybe the game had run overtime?

Finally, just as your knees couldn't bear the hard floor anymore, a woman arrived. Wrapped in a towel, she turned the shower on and waited until the water became warm and steam clouds began to fill the room.

'I'm glad the team had an away game, aren't you? Let's us coaches get together.'

You couldn't see who she was calling out to, but you then understood why the showers had been empty until now. It didn't matter that the rest were away, it looked like you were still going to get your long-awaited, real-time porn show. Did she have to shower facing the wall though, and why was the room so steamy? It was making it hard to see her.

'Are you coming in? The water's hot now, and so am I.'

Who was she talking to and what did she mean? She turned slowly, rubbing soap over her breasts, pinching her nipples between her fingers. Your hand slid down to your crotch, and feeling yourself harden, you undid your belt buckle so you could rub yourself properly. If only the morons could see you now. They'd love to be seeing this show, but thankfully they weren't.

As she turned her back to the hole in the wall, another person came in. 'Finally,' she squealed with pleasure. The steam was getting too thick; it was getting even harder to see. The other person joined the woman and she leaned back into their arms. She started to moan. You wished they'd turn around; all you could see were their butts. The moaning intensified and the other person was rubbing her lower down, down there. You looked down at your pecker. It was hard and shiny and your hand was moving backward and forward. It felt good. Your mother had told you not to put your hands in your trousers, it was wrong – although you weren't sure why. And the morons were always talking about wanking. You had to look the word up in the library and the book said it was normal for boys to do . . . but you were getting distracted. You didn't want thoughts of your mother interrupting this precious moment. You carried on rubbing back and forth, bringing your eye back to the hole. The couple had turned right round and the woman was facing your way. Her hands were running through the other person's short hair but you couldn't see who it was, only the top of his head. You didn't care. This was one amazing show. An arm was coming from behind the woman, rubbing her fast between her legs at the front, while another hand was squeezing a breast. Her eyes were rolling back in her head and she looked as if she was about to have a fit, as she moved rhythmically to the hand. She let out a long, gurgled moan and then a satisfied smile and turned to the other person, just as you, too, felt a warm rush and a release. Your hand was wet and you were exhausted, but you felt brilliant.

'Now your turn,' the woman crooned in delight, turning to face her partner.

'No, hun, not this time, I'm running late. I'll catch you in the staff room tomorrow . . .'

You didn't hear the woman's reply. There was a loud buzzing in your ears and the cupboard suddenly felt hot and claustrophobic. You couldn't breathe. The other person was another woman. You heard their voice and only then realised that they too had woman's titties and a triangle of pubic hair. Her hair was cut short, boyish, and she'd been behind the other woman, so you hadn't noticed the lack of male bits. Bile welled up at the back of your throat, burning to get out. Lumpy, brown and orange vomit splashed over your trousers and shoes as you fell back from the hole. This was your punishment. You hastily dragged the back of your hand across your mouth, wiping away any residual spew. You needed air and so started to do back up your fly with your wet, sticky fingers.

It was only then you noticed the crack of light at the cupboard door and the watching silhouettes.

CHAPTER ONE

Jinny

I knew I was embarking on a new and different path when I got a ludicrously fucking high score in the 'Are You A White Witch?' quiz in the gossip mag. Still, I didn't expect a week later, to be freezing my tits off in two degrees Celsius, naked in my backyard, chanting in the middle of a bloody chalk-drawn pentagon. Fuck knows how I was going to erase the chalk marks before Fiona saw it, but I'd worry about that later. Right now, though, I had to visualise my desire firmly in my mind's eye, recite the spell I'd conjured up, burn the paper with my desire on it, and send it into the universe to manifest. I could barely speak, far less chant because my teeth were chattering like a pair of castanets and my feet were so blue, it felt like my toes might snap off in the bloody ridiculous flip-flops I had on. The wind whipped my hair in my face as I held my spell in one hand and a glass with a candle in the other. The moon was full, it had to be for the spell, but it was only visible through the gaps in the threatening rain clouds. With the candle held up to

6

the paper, both for light and ceremonial purposes, I was just able to make out my writing. Luckily, I remembered most of it. With the chanting bit over, I was about to burn the paper and the bloody candle blew out. I turned to get a light from another candle and the rest of them, the other five, had all been blown out too. Shite. What sort of pathetic newbie witch was I? This was way harder than I thought it would be. My body was stiff with the cold as I bent to relight them all and start again. I'd have to be faster this time. I didn't want to jinx the spell by not having them lit.

I regretted not tying my hair up as it obscured my vision. When I planned this, I had this wonderful impression of a beautiful, naked woman standing in all her glory under the moonlight, hair flowing. Of course, that didn't take into account the bloody weather. I relit each candle in turn, praying there were no neighbours having a sleepless night, or they'd have got more than they bargained for, looking out of their window. My white arse on show was not the full moon they'd be expecting. All candles lit again, I quickly chanted the spell and set fire to the paper with the candle I was holding. Using my body to shield it from the wind, it burned successfully. Too successfully, as I burned my bloody fingers holding on to it until all the writing had turned to ash. Extinguished, I let the last bit of blank paper fly off, blew out each candle in turn and gathered them up as I ran inside the kitchen door before I froze to the spot.

Finally warm again, wrapped in a fleecy blanket over my pjs, and a cup of chamomile tea in hand, I questioned my sanity. I was a desperate woman. Desperate women took desperate measures. I'd tried everything else. Was I blowing everything out of proportion? Our fight tonight was downright nasty and potentially fatal for our relationship, but what was I to do? If I didn't talk out, or act on my suspicions, I was going to lose her. I had to take the risk. I drank the rest of my tea. Thawed now, I went back up to bed. Fiona was turned to the window, so sneaking into bed and keeping my stone-cold feet away from her would be easy. She always left before me in the morning, so that'd give me plenty of time to clean up the chalk drawing outside. Too cold still to sleep, I lay awake for at least an hour before I eventually quieted my worried mind enough to submit to oblivion.

***

Ally was already sitting at their normal table by the time Jinny joined her for lunch.

'You're late,' Ally complained. Putting her newspaper aside she nodded to the waitress. 'I got your usual.'

'Cheers. I had stuff to do before I left. It took longer than I thought it would.'

'It couldn't have waited till later? You know I don't have long for lunch.'

'No, I had to get something cleaned up before Fiona got back.'

'You two still fighting? I suspected something was up when the swear box app was pinging non-stop.'

Jinny had designed and sold a swear box phone app that automatically picked up on swear words, debited a small fine from users and allocated it to a designated account. 'I'm blo– blinking trying. Really I am, but you know what I'm like when I'm stressed.'

'At this rate we'll be able to holiday in the

Caribbean at your expense sooner than we'd hoped.'

'Yeah, well it turned a bit nasty.' A waitress slid a bowl of soup in front of Jinny and left. 'Thanks Linda,' Jinny shouted after her. Taking a deep breath, she faced Ally and her judgment. 'We had a real blo– blowout last night.' The rich aroma of garlic and tomatoes were acknowledged with a hungry tummy rumble.

'You realise you're going to drive her away with your jealousy.' Ally interrupted Jinny's enjoyment of the moment. 'You need to trust her.'

'I can't sit back without a fight, Ally. I just can't.'

'Well, I think your paranoia is going to drive her away.'

Jinny rolled her eyes. She knew Ally would say that. 'I'm not being paranoid. She's given him access to the bank account, given him access to all our secure drives. Showed him all the proposed work and what we get paid for it. This isn't stuff you should be showing to an employee.'

'Isn't it? Maybe it is. Doesn't Kevin need all that access if he's dealing with clients' accounts?'

'No. He's a computer programmer. He's employed to program, not fuc– not run the company. That's Fiona's and my job. We only took him on because the workload was getting too big for us both to handle. He was just for support. But now Fiona spends every blo– blinking working hour in the office, with him. Before we hired him, we mostly worked at home together. I feel like I'm being excluded.' Jinny sighed heavily, and stirred her soup that was getting colder by the minute.

'Look, sis, I think you're reading too much into it. I mean, after all, Fiona's gay. And she probably hired a male employee so you *won't* get jealous. Maybe she's going to the office to guide him. Why

9

don't you take it in turns to do that?'

'I offered that, but Fiona said she wanted to get out of the house more. And since the office is only big enough for two, where does that leave me?'

'Have you told her about your concerns about giving him access to confidential information, then?'

'That's what last night's bomb was about. She got all defensive about it. Said Kev needed access to do his job from start to finish–'

'See–'

'But I explained that it wasn't his role.' Jinny took some mouthfuls of rapidly cooling soup. 'Where's your lunch?' she asked Ally, just noticing that she was eating alone.

'I've finished. I told you. You were late.' Ally grabbed the roll she knew Jinny wouldn't eat and started nibbling at it.

Jinny noticed a queue forming at the till, and a flustered Linda trying to take payment, while the cook, Jez, was shouting out orders ready to go.

'Shit. I'll be back in a minute,' she told Ally and headed over to the till.

'Where's Roz?' she asked Linda.

'Stock-taking, in the back.'

Jinny pushed through the double doors, nodding to Jez as she passed the kitchen. In the backroom Linda was going through the stock, ticking it off on her clipboard.

'Roz?' Roz jumped. 'Leave this to the quieter times. There's a queue out front and Linda can't manage on her own.'

'Okay. Sure, Jinny. It wasn't busy when I started.'

'This can be done anytime, Roz. You know it's getting more and more mobbed since across the road closed down.'

'On it. It won't happen again.'

'It's fine. I just don't want to lose staff if they feel they can't cope. If it keeps getting busier and we need more staff, let me know.'

'Okay. I'll monitor the situation and let you know. You ever coming back?'

'I don't know, Roz. Work with Fiona's really busy. But I hired you because I knew you could run the place fine on your own.'

'Made an ass of it today though, didn't I?'

'Don't be an ass. Hah! As you said, it was quiet when you started. Linda should've let you know she needed help. So don't worry about it.'

Jinny followed Roz out the room and left her to her job as cafe manager and went back to Ally.

'Trouble in paradise?'

'Nah, it's fine. So where were we?'

'I said you were being paranoid . . . as normal.'

'Let's say I'm not being paranoid. What's your advice? What if she really is having an affair? She hasn't touched me in over a month. And if I try to get close to her, she makes some excuse to get away. Now if that isn't suspicious, tell me what is?'

Ally sighed and shrugged. 'I've known you both for too long to give you proper advice. I just see you jumping to conclusions and blowing things way out of proportion, like you normally do. As I said, she's not into guys, so why would she be having an affair with Kevin? See, I can't give you unbiased advice.'

'Well, pretend a client came to you for counselling with what I've told you. What would you say to her?' Jinny finished off her cold soup as she watched Ally sit back and think about it.

'Look, if it were a client, I would offer them joint counselling for their relationship. You've already said Fiona wasn't interested in talking, as she said you're the one with the problem, not her. So I can't advise. But I know you, and I'd say she was probably right–'

Jinny was about to accuse her sister of not being supportive, but Ally held her hand up so she could finish.

'However, if you still think you have just cause for feeling the way you do, explain to her how *you* feel and ask her to help you. Explain to her what you told me, that you miss her touch. Ask her if there is something you can do, both of you, to bridge the gap. Talk.'

Jinny knew Ally was right. Their argument last night had been straight into accusations and defense. They really needed to sit down and talk about it. 'Okay. I'll talk to her tonight.'

Ally stuffed the last bit of roll into her mouth and muffled her response. 'Ah eeh oo ho. Ot a ien ah un.' Totally understood by Jinny as 'I've got to go. Got a client at one.' Quite often they didn't need to talk to know what the other was saying. It had always been like that. It used to annoy the hell out of their family, but they'd mastered the art of speaking without consonants.

Jinny watched her sister leave, feeling a bit better now she'd got that off her chest. She motioned to Linda to bring her a coffee, and took her laptop out. She stared at the database in front of her, her mind wandering. She closed her laptop. Work just wasn't happening today. She accepted the coffee from Linda who smiled her thanks for taking the pressure off earlier. Now she just had to think about what she would say tonight to get Fiona to listen to her concerns without shutting her down.

CHAPTER TWO

Ally

There it was, that 'black dog' pressing down on me, darkening my mood – again. What was it? The cutting, wet wind that had me pulling my heavy, dark, military style coat around me tighter; my sister's current relationship woes or because I was heading back to work? Probably all of them, but at least I knew the weather would improve, eventually. I couldn't be sure that my sister's relationship problems or my feelings about my job would be any better in the foreseeable future.

Listening to Jinny describing her latest love saga was just as painful and upsetting as having my fingernails pulled out one by one, whilst I drank my coffee. Or maybe more so; it was that gruesome. She always seemed to be able to take a regular situation and bend it all out of shape, until her world was collapsing in on her. And why, oh why couldn't anyone else in her world see it too? She never bloody listened to my advice, so I don't know why she even asked for it.

The wet pavements glistened in the low, wintery sunshine as I walked the short route back to work. How long till it started pissing again? I lifted my face, feeling the sun's warmth for as long as it stayed clear, nodding my head to the passers-by that I regularly encountered living in this small town.

I liked it here, despite the rain. I came here from the city, to be closer to Jinny, after I split from my last relationship. It felt as if I had lost a piece of myself when Anthony and I parted, even though it was a mutual agreement. There just wasn't that spark anymore with him. What was the point? We bravely moved on, but living with someone for over ten years meant I needed a sense of family, closeness, someone that knew me, warts and all, to see the lonely nights through, so I came here and ended up staying. Here, with its small, clean, narrow streets, friendly upmarket cafes and shops, felt like home now. Jinny had since moved to the next town, a few miles along, but we still managed to see each other most days at her café.

I loved Jinny, as infuriating as she was. She and Fiona were great together; I truly hoped she didn't bugger things up between them. Why don't people talk? Why do they let fears and worries into the cracks of their relationships instead of communicating? I shook my head as I pushed open the door to the counselling centre.

The centre was bright and modern, designed to help lift the moods of those that needed its services, whilst comfortable consulting rooms furnished with large cushioned sofas and coffee tables coaxed clients into relaxing and letting go of their problems. Sharon, our lone administrator, looked up from her keyboard and smiled over the rim of her multi-coloured glasses. Her look and dress were a mishmash of styles thrown together, which strangely worked for her. She called herself a fashionista, whatever that was. I knew that, had I dressed as she did, I'd look like Lady Gaga on steroids. I liked Sharon; she was reliable, extremely efficient and, despite her crazy, colourful demeanour, her understanding nods and homely attitude brought a sense of calmness to her surroundings.

'Your two o'clock's here.' Sharon's eyes looked to the man in the waiting area. He had arrived early, so she'd already served him a coffee from the filter pot that simmered all day in the corner, giving off a sharp, acrid whiff of stale, burnt coffee.

'Thanks Sharon.' I removed my coat and looked in the mirror. Jeez. I'd only been outside for ten minutes and my hair looked like the stuffing on a burst couch. I straightened it quickly with my fingers and reapplied my lipstick. I was roughly five feet four, with shoulder-length, natural, reddish-brown hair and a slim frame. I had been a bit of an ugly duckling when I hit puberty, feeling gawky and uncomfortable in my own skin, but over the years the awkwardness faded, leaving me feeling happy with how I looked. I wasn't stunning, I enhanced my eyes and cheeks with a touch of make-up to add some colour to my pale skin, but I'd caught enough appreciative male looks to know I was attractive.

'Mr Colson? I'm Ally, one of the counsellors. Please come in.' He hadn't touched his coffee. I couldn't blame him; one sip of it would have left his mouth tasting like the dregs of a sick bowl. I directed him to one of the counselling rooms and he eased himself onto the dark grey sofa. 'Weather's not so good today. Did you manage to find the centre okay?'

'Erm, yes. I used the satnav.' He looked uncomfortable, despite the usual rapport-building chat supposed to help clients feel more at ease, before they bled their weary hearts out in the counselling session.

'Thank you for filling out the form. Although we get a referral from your doctor, it is good to get a feel for why you think counselling may help and what you want to get from our sessions. Is that ok, Mr Colson? Do you mind if I call you Frederick?'

'Eh, yes. It's Fred, I prefer Fred, thanks.' He shifted uneasily, probably wishing we could just get over the polite exchanges and start dealing with the nitty-gritty of why he was here.

'Okay, why don't you tell me what's led you to this point. Am I right your wife passed away a short time ago? I'm sorry for your lo–'

His hands came up to cradle his face and he started sobbing. Deep sobs, the kind that shake your body to the core. It was going to be a long session . . .

***

I loved my job. I loved helping people, but the never-ending cycle of sad, desperate stories were taking their toll on my own sanity. Was every human being on this dying planet sitting on the precipice of their own mental demise? The centre's waiting list was growing every day with sad people needing an outlet for their inner demons. Maybe I just needed a holiday. I gazed at the natural landscapes pinned to the wall: lakes, mountains, glorious sunsets in green pastures drew my imagination and desire to escape into the frame. How do you persuade a grieving man, whose whole life was wrapped, coddled and directed by his wife, to start living again? The session had drained me.

'Ally, Dr Garby's on line one.' Sharon's

interruption dragged me from my imaginary dreamscape.

'Dr Garby, Gill, how are you? It's been a while since we met for a drink.'

'Hi Ally. I'm good, thanks. I know, let's get together soon. I've a referral for you. It's a tricky one.'

'Oh, okay. Let me grab a pen to take some quick notes until you send over the referral letter. It'll let me get the paperwork started.' Tricky. My heart sank. What next? What torture had this poor soul been through? 'Right. I'm ready. What's the client's name, Gill?'

'It's Anne Bishopton . . .' She paused. She knew I'd know the name right way. Anne Bishopton was the owner of the local hotel, The Gables. She and her husband, Bill, ran it together, along with a generous staff. The hotel was always busy, mainly because it attracted countless salespeople who trailed through the many closely strung towns; they got a place to rest their head at a reasonable price and a homely feel. It also had a cosy snug where working couples could filter out of their office jobs and into the hotel for a pub meal and a glass of wine. I tended to avoid going there. Watching folk snog in dimly lit corners was not appealing to me in my current unattached status.

'Don't worry, Gill, it's a confidential service. But before you tell me the reason for referral, would Anne be happy talking to someone that lives locally?'

'I already checked. Yep, she's fine with that, but she doesn't want her husband to know. She left him a couple of nights ago, after he gave her a black eye and two cracked ribs.'

'Oh no. So it's not just town gossip that Bill Bishopton beats his wife after one too many?'

'No, not just gossip. It was becoming a common

occurrence. I've asked her in the past if he abused her, but she strongly denied it, pretended to be shocked at the suggestion.'

'I guess there's only so much a person can take – or was it just too difficult to hide the truth?'

'Well, to be honest, I think she has her sister, Debbie, to thank for literally dragging her out of the hotel. She went to visit, saw Anne's bruises, and told Bill that if he came near her again, he'd get a dose of his own medicine. Debbie was the one that contacted me, too. To check her injuries, make sure she was okay.'

'Good for Debbie. Thank God Anne has someone to support her. Where is she staying, Gill? At Debbie's?'

'Yeah, for now . . . but Debbie has so many kids and I kinda picked up that things were a bit cramped, not to mention Debbie's hubby isn't too keen on Anne being there. He never saw eye to eye with Bill, knew he was a wife beater.'

'Is she pressing charges?'

'No. The police had him in. Cautioned him. It's all they can do.'

'Sounds like she could do with a referral to the refuge, at least until she can get on her feet. I'll contact the minister, let him know she might need a space.'

'Are you sure, Ally? I can do it – it's no problem.'

'It's okay, Gill. I need to contact him anyway, to check on another client.'

Gill and I continued to work through the referral, going over the mundane details required for the forms. Another broken mind, body and spirit; I'd provide the counselling ear to help heal the unseen wounds. My grandfather always said talking over your problems was good for the soul. It was probably in a moment of childhood anguish that he spoke those words to me, I couldn't remember the exact memory, but his kind words stayed with me. I believed him. Being an introvert at school, I always seemed to attract the broken kids, the ones that needed someone to listen to their woes. I became good at listening, observing, and a natural at advising, without preaching, letting the person find their own solutions. It was a natural progression to complete a master's degree in counselling psychology.

My last task for the day was to contact the women's refuge to make sure they had a space for Anne if she needed it; it sounded likely. And I'd have no problems in recommending she go there. The refuge, simply called The Old Manse, was situated about three miles outside of town and secluded in peaceful woodlands. It was an excellent hideaway and peaceful retreat for battered, abused wives and their children, having a devoted staff team, headed up by the town's minister and a deputy. All were female, except John Proctor, the minister, who founded the place; being male didn't seem to matter though, as he was more often than not their first port of call when things became desperate at home. He did a lot for the community, regardless of religious denomination and his kind, non-judgemental attitude meant he was often the first person sought out to set up various community-led groups and events.

Tired, but keen to make sure Anne would not be left without a place to turn to, or God forbid, feel she had to return home, I dialled the minister's number.

'Reverend Proctor. How can I help you?'

'John, it's Ally. I may have another client in need of a place at The Manse.'

19

Jinny

I sat in the car outside the house, taking deep breaths and working up the courage to ask Fiona if we could have a calm and coherent talk tonight. The house was lit up like an amusement park, telling me she was home already. Fiona could afford to burn electricity.

The house was hers, handed down to her through generations. A beautiful, old sandstone building, it stood three storeys tall, surrounded by a hectare of mature gardens and ancient trees. It made sense that I'd move in with her four years ago. We'd already been together for six years and we had built our software company together, running it from the house. But, as I looked now at the formidable building, much as I admired its beauty, it never felt like home. It never felt like *my* home. I liked minimalist, Fiona liked traditional. I wanted to redecorate, Fiona liked it as it was. But I loved her, so I settled for whatever she wanted. And we *were* happy, until three months ago when she fucking employed Kevin. Then everything changed. She became distant and blamed it on the stresses of the company, but refused to let me do more. Of course, she had a masters in business on top of her computing degree, so she employed Kev and then assumed the responsibility to manage him. Plus, my forte was in software design and development, as she loved to remind me, when I offered to help in the office. Like the house, I felt detached, detached from our work, from her.

The light in the kitchen came on, adding an orange glow to the mist that had settled in the garden. I turned the engine off and decided to delay the confrontation no longer.

'Oh good, you're just in time. Set the table will you? Dinner's ready.' Fiona drained the pasta as I put the glass mats – my only allowed contribution to the décor of the antique pine kitchen diner – on the ancient wooden table.

'How was the office?' I didn't want to jump right in with our relationship troubles. Maybe let the wine take effect first. Mellow her out a bit.

'The usual,' Fiona said dismissively. 'Did you finish that database for Chemomeds?'

'Not yet. The café was busy, so I helped out.'

Fiona looked at me, debating whether or not to argue. I knew she wanted me to finish that job as soon as possible, so I'd be free for other work, but she also knew we had over a week till the deadline and I only had a day or two's work left on it. She nodded and poured the tomato and garlic sauce over the pasta. It looked and smelt delicious but my appetite was absent, stressing about the conversation I wanted to have. I watched her toned body, in tight, black jeans and fitted tee, move about the kitchen. Damn, she had a bloody great arse. I twisted the cap off the cabernet sauvignon I'd brought home with me and poured us both a glass. We ate in silence. We never used to. Meal times used to be buzzing with ideas for our business, or we'd have a laugh at whatever conspiracy theory Ally had been regaling that day. I tried to break the tension.

'The swear box app is doing well. I've got over thirty-five thousand downloads and some more great five-star reviews.'

'That's good. I'm glad you did it. It should bring you in a tidy sum as it becomes more popular.'

My hackles rose at the suggestion of the app

being a separate venture from our business. Fiona felt mobile apps should be a different branch from our other software products, so she was adamant that I set it up as my own company. I thought she was being generous at the time, but now I just bloody wondered if she was ensuring if we ever split, I'd have my clients and mobile app business while she retained her clients and the software end of things. Or was that me being paranoid, reading into things that weren't there? Maybe Ally was right. I was getting as bad as her at conspiracies. I finished my meal in silence.

'I'm going to Zumba tonight.' Fiona broke into my thoughts on how I would bring up us again, without it escalating like last night.

'What? After half a bottle of wine?' I laughed.

'Kevin's picking me up. It's just to give it a recce. I might not like it.'

I gritted my jaws in an attempt not to reply. Kevin again. Fuck. Images of them naked and screwing flooded into my head.

'I was hoping we could have a talk. Try clear up the mess from last night–'

'Jeez. Let's not go there again, Jinny. I've already told you, I'm not having an affair with my employee. Just because I'm going to Zumba with him, doesn't mean you should be reading anything into it.'

'I know, I know. I was just wanting to clear the air–'

'I can't go through the same conversation over and over again wi–'

'That's what I wanted to say. I wanted to apologise. I'm sorry, Fiona. I'm just frightened . . . frightened you'll leave me. I feel so excluded with you being in the office so much–'

'Can we leave it? I need to get ready. And I can't

deal with any more jealousy. I've had enough of it.'

'I know. I trust you, Fi. Please forgive me. Maybe we can talk later about what we can do together? Just so I don't feel excluded.'

'There's nothing to talk about.' Fiona stood up, cheeks flushed from the wine and her disapproval.

This wasn't working out the way I'd planned it. I was losing the battle again and I did feel guilty that it was me. Was it all my fault? Fiona stormed off, stamping hard on the way upstairs. I poured another glass of wine and wondered where it was all going so wrong.

She left without saying anything. I tidied up the kitchen, drank the rest of the bottle of wine while watching some crime documentary, and by the time I went to bed at eleven Fiona was still not back. My racing heart kept me awake till nearly two in the morning when I heard her come in. I pretended I was asleep when she sneaked into bed, smelling of vanilla from the shower she'd just had.

She's showering because she was at Zumba, I reassured myself.

I did promise myself to have a sniff of her clothes tomorrow for unknown scents, though. Maybe the crime documentary was playing on my mind, making me paranoid, so I re-negotiated with myself that I would definitely *not* fucking sniff her clothes. Ally would be so angry with me for even thinking it.

***

Ally

'Morning Ally. Not so nice today, eh?'

That was the third person to mention the

weather as they passed. It was raining – again. I didn't need to be reminded every five, bloody seconds. Stop it, Ally, I scolded myself. People are just trying to be nice. *Smile.* I hadn't even started work yet and I was already a miserable bitch. I looked up to the sky. Maybe that rain was full of mind depressing, chemical shit. It wouldn't surprise me. God knows what chemicals we were being polluted by. If Jinny were here, she'd no doubt be laughing and calling me a conspiracy theorist and I'd be arguing back, saying that the term 'conspiracy theory' was used by those that knew damn well what was going on, to make people look like quacks.

I pushed open the centre's door. It was like bloody Groundhog Day. What heart-wrenching, stomach-churning delights awaited me today? I spotted Anne Bishopton and her sister Debbie in the waiting area. Anne had sunglasses on, to cover the bruises on her eyes; hiding from potential embarrassment. It was her husband that should feel embarrassed, not her. But I understood. Who wants to advertise the fact that they are living with the devil and are too scared and vulnerable to leave? I hung up my coat, got some fresh water for the counselling room and made sure that the hankie box had plenty of tissues in it.

'Anne, Debbie, please come, sit down.' I gestured to the sofas as I led them into the counselling room.

'I haven't seen you both for a while.' I didn't want to ask how they were. People couldn't help but answer 'fine', even when their world had imploded and they were in the middle of a shit-storm.

'No, it has been a while.' Debbie answered for both of them just as Anne put her head down and began weeping. I guessed she'd been holding in the anguish for too long and in this safe place she broke, letting out the grief.

'I'm sorry, Anne, things have been very hard on you. I'm glad, though, that you've found the strength to come in today.' I pushed the hankie box closer as teardrops flowed down her cheeks and mingled with clear snot at the end of her nose. Her sister put her arm around her and tried to comfort her. It felt awkward.

'Debbie, I can see you've been a great support for Anne. I think what is best for her, is if Anne and I could have this time to just go over some things. You could wait or come back in an hour?'

Debbie looked concerned, I knew she was worried that her sister would not tell the truth on her own, but I had to take the risk. I wanted Anne to open up to me without worrying what Debbie thought. As close as they were, it was personal, private and raw.

'Er, okay.' Debbie patted her sister. 'Is that okay with you, Anne?'

'She'll be fine, Debbie, I promise.' I stood up before waiting for Anne's reply and guided Debbie out.

'Anne, this is a safe place. All you tell me is between us, no one else. Tell me what happened. It's not the first time Bill has hurt you, is it?'

'He . . . he wasn't always like this. He used to be a good man. Now this is gonna be all that people see. Me . . . beaten up . . . and him . . . him a wife beater. Debbie shouldn't have told the doctor. I know she was just trying to help . . . but it's worse now. It's embarrass–'

'You said he wasn't always like this. What changed, Anne?' I interrupted her tirade, trying to get her to refocus.

'It . . . it was my f . . . fault.' She began sobbing

again.

'Anne, domestic violence is never the victim's fault. Never.'

'He caught me. It was years ago, not long after we had moved to Spain, when Bill took that hotel manager's job. We hadn't been married long. I was young, naïve, drunk. I let some guy kiss me at a wedding reception and Bill saw us. He beat the guy up, threw him out. It was the first time he hit me. I'll never forget it . . . I deserved it.'

'Violence is never right, Anne. You were young, you'd been drinking.'

'He's become more jealous over the years – even though I've never given him any reason to be. I learned my lesson. I thought that moving back here would help. Y' know, settle him, but if anything, he just seems more angry, more abusive.' She blew her nose, trying to control her breathing, trying to stop the sobbing, but years of misery had welled up inside her, waiting for this moment to break free.

'You moved back here when Bill's parents retired, didn't you?' I questioned, trying to find a focus away from the grief.

'Yes, they wanted to retire to France and Bill thought it'd be nice to come home again, manage the hotel and build up a nest egg for when we retire. That was about eight years ago.' Anne calmed down and we began to focus on a therapy plan.

Our counselling session overran; I wanted Anne to believe she was not to blame. She had no lessons to learn, other than learning how to leave an abusive partner. She carried so much guilt, especially as she knew Gill Garby would be reporting him to the police. I had to gauge how she'd feel about going to the women's refuge. It didn't look promising. Some women never leave their partner, unless it's in a box.

Bill had certainly done a good job over the years, making her feel useless, weak, unable to live without him. Men, even some women, can become expert manipulators – or do they just manage to pick out the most vulnerable of partners?

Debbie was still there, in the waiting room. Sharon had served her a cup of our acid coffee, which unsurprisingly, still sat in front of her, looking cold, stale and even less appealing, if that was even possible. She looked up from her dog-eared magazine, probably wondering - no, hoping - that Anne had worked through her woes and was now stronger. But reality was never that easy. Sometimes it took years for people to change their minds, sometimes never.

'I'll wait in the car for you,' Anne mumbled, clearly wanting to escape any prying eyes and awkward pleasantries that may await her in the street.

'Thanks for bringing her in, Debbie. You've been a great support.'

'I'm her sister, isn't that what sisters are supposed to do?'

'I'm a counsellor, I know all the right things to say and do, yet even I don't feel as if I'm able to support my own sister just now.'

'Oh, is Jinny okay? She's a lovely girl. You both are.'

'She's fine, Debbie. She probably just needs someone less biased than her own sister to give her advice. I know her too well.'

'I know what you mean. It's hard not to sound too preachy when you give advice to friends or family. Anne can be the worst for listening. That's why I encouraged her to see you. Maybe Jinny could join a group?'

'A group? Er, I'm not sure she needs anything too deep. We all go through these sorts of stresses. It's pretty normal. I mean she's not distressed in any way. More just annoyed at how she's been treated.'

'Oh, of course. I really just meant a group of like-minded folk that she could chat with, take her mind off the situation. A distraction, sort of,' Debbie explained but I wasn't really sure what she was getting at.

'Look, I don't normally tell anyone about this, but . . .' Debbie looked around and moved in closer, to almost whisper, '. . . I'm a witch.'

'What? Like Sabrina?' I replied without thinking, taken aback by her statement.

'Oh, please.' She rolled her eyes.

How often had someone said that to her? I felt bad. I'm an open-minded person, I believe in lots of alternative stuff. Hell, I even believe in UFOs. I mean how likely is it that we are alone on this tiny blue, green planet in this enormous universe? But, witchy stuff? The notion conjured up images of naked men and women with overgrown pubes, dancing around a fire in the woods and then having orgies. I'd obviously watched too many atrocious seventies horror movies.

'I'm sorry. What? Erm, you're a witch?'

'I know it sounds mad, way out there, not the sort of thing you hear a lot.' Debbie shrugged. 'But really, we're just a small group who like helping people. We're looking for new members to join our coven. We're discreet. New members can only join through the recommendation from another member. I thought . . . I just thought maybe you and Jinny might like to come along?'

'I'm not sure it's my . . . or even Jinny's sort of thing–'

'Look, you said Jinny needed some support. She's gay, isn't she? Surely, support from an alternative group might be just what she needs, and there are other gays there too. It's not just about our art, we're about healing, talking, trying to work out how to live in this insane world. Well, we're a mixed group. Really inclusive – and we're looking for various types of occupations, ones that can help the group. You being a counsellor would be great.'

'I'm not sure–'

'Don't say anything. Just think about it. There's a meeting in a couple of nights' time at The Towers. We meet at eight.' She opened her bag, rummaged around and pulled out a leaflet which she discreetly pushed into my hand.

'The details are in there. Come, see for yourself.'

'The Towers? Nasir and Amira Bamra's place? You have witchy get-togethers at their place?'

'No one knows it's a coven. We're just a support group, as far as anyone is concerned. The Bamras do a lot for the community, but they host this, as well. Look, if we see you there, great. If not, please don't mention it to anyone. I'd better get on. Anne's waiting.'

'I wouldn't say anything. I'll talk to Jinny. Take care, Debbie. And thanks.'

I watched her go out, into the rain. Witches, I thought, who knew? Witches in Covenston.

CHAPTER THREE

There you see her, there she is. Fucking, filthy whore. This is it, you'll show her and she'll understand now, that dirty cunt. Once you've changed her, you'll free her of this burden and she'll be glad.

You're so good at this. Taking the time to get the job done right. Your patience and stealth has paid off because tonight's the big night. It's not been easy following the bitch around, it never is, there's always the risk that you'll be seen. But people are so complacent these days. They relax into their routines. They're like fucking robots doing the same thing day in, day out. Building her diary was easy for you, just a matter of picking the best place for the big event. Everyday you've watched her go from work, to the shops, visit her mother at the residential home and other equally, mundane trips. It's a no-brainer that it'd be here, though. The gym. This would be the place; on the outskirts of town where they've stolen some of the green belt to build various recreation centres; surrounded by trees, and quiet walkways that no one ever walks. Fuck, she's made it even easier for you by parking at the far off corner so that no one will damage her precious Mercedes. You'll show the uppity cunt now.

She usually takes an hour and a half. That gives her time to use the equipment, pool and sauna. You know this because you saw her in there. You saw her cavorting with them. The evil's inside her. She's in there again now. Flirting around while she works up a sweat in skimpy clothing. She'll shower for you, good. And she'll be tired from the exercise. That's why you'll wait till afterwards, easier to take her down, especially as the bitch likes to keep fit. Can't have her trying to fight you off. No, you've got it all planned beautifully. Doesn't matter how long she takes, it'll give you time to picture the scene, play it over, imagine how she'll respond, plan for any mishaps. There won't be any. You're too good at this.

There are not many cars left now. She'll be out soon. Time to get into position. You can feel it, can't you? Your strength, building inside, gaining momentum from the adrenaline surge. Your dedication, your passion, for this act; making them over, fixing their damage. Someone needs to do it – and that's you. You were fucking born for this. This is your legacy.

She's out. Your focus is intense. Like an eagle, focused solely on its prey, waiting until that perfect moment to pounce. That moment where they'll be off guard, unsuspecting. It'll be so easy, she's busy looking for her car keys. She has no fucking idea. Here goes. Hood over her head from behind. You've got her. She's like a confused rabbit, wondering what the fuck has just happened in her oh-so-fucking, pretty mundane life. Wondering why. Tighten the rope on the hood. Just enough to knock her out. Just enough so you can gag and tie her. You've got her. Ha . . . and off to dreamland, pretty one.

With every thrust, every stab, you fix the lie. It's

your mantra now. You made up a wee tune that you sing to go along with the words. You sang it when you fixed the first one all those years ago. And you've perfected your skill since then. Some you keep awake, others, the fitter, stronger ones, you knock out. Just like this sleeping cunt . . . She's stirring now. You hold there till you feel her wake, tense, realise you are there to help her. Moaning as she feels you in her wetness. You're ready now to thrust. Take your time, let her feel it. She wants you to change her. It's the evil inside her that is struggling against you. And when you've finished your act, she'll know she's different. She'll know you fixed her and you can scratch another name from your list.

CHAPTER FOUR

Ally

I was walking along the beach, arm in arm with my gran. Our feet were bare and the sea felt cold as it lapped over our toes. I was distracted by the way the sand had formed ripples, which felt lumpy under my feet, and the sun was so bright I couldn't look properly ahead without my eyes blurring with tears - or was I crying? I couldn't remember. I couldn't remember what my gran had just told me and I struggled to see her face, to hear what she was saying . . . it was just so bright. I wanted to hear, but when I finally focused on her mouth, it was open wide and a strange noise was coming out. A shrill, piercing noise as she held her mouth open. Confusion slid over me and it became dark. I wanted to hear what my gran was saying but the scene was slipping away, while the noise became louder, more intense . . . until I realised that I was being dragged from a dream by the sound of my mobile.

'H . . . h . . . hello.' My throat was so dry I could barely speak and I felt so bloody groggy. Dragged out of a deep REM cycle while getting advice, or trying to, from dear old, dead gran was not conducive to a good start.

'Can I speak with Ms Canessa . . . Ms Alison Canessa?'

'Yes . . . sp– speaking.' I raised myself up unto my elbow to somehow try to feel more awake. 'This is Ally, who is this?'

'Ally, it's Michelle at the A&E. I'm sorry it's so early.'

My blurry eyes strained to see the numbers on the bedside clock glow 4.25 a.m. There was usually only one reason for an early call from the hospital.

'There's been a rape, Ally. The police asked me to call you.'

'Oh, right. I'll get there as soon as I can. Which Inspector is on duty this morning, Michelle?'

'It's the new guy, erm . . . Detective Chief Inspector Daniels. Nick Daniels. He seems nice.'

'Let him know I'm on my way.'

'Will do. She'll be in recovery area by the time you get here, Ally.'

'Recovery? Oh, right, I'll go there then.' I'd find out the details soon enough, I guessed, not wanting to delay getting there any more than necessary.

A rape, as I suspected, when the phone rang at this ungodly hour. It was my job to see the victim as soon as possible, for support, guidance, a friendly face. The face they would see, for as long as they needed, to get through the trauma - if they ever did. The *victim*. I hated that word. It gave power to the perpetrator. Some people preferred survivor but that still didn't sit right with me, it still felt wrong.

There were no adequate words to describe the scene that awaited at the hospital either. There were police everywhere. This wasn't normal for a rape case; something more had happened. I showed my lanyard badge to the officer at the department door and was directed to the charge nurse's room, off the main corridor. It wasn't a large room to begin with, but it felt unbearably cramped with the numerous people that were discussing the case. Everyone looked up as I entered.

'Ally, thanks for coming in so quickly. Everyone this is Ally – eh, Alison Canessa, the counsellor.' Michelle, the nurse from the A&E, directed me to her chair. 'Ally, you sit here and the Inspector can explain what has happened. I'll get back down to A&E now. If anyone needs me, you know where to find me.'

Michelle left me feeling alone and uncomfortable in a sea of unfamiliar faces.

'Ms Canessa, thanks for coming in. I wish we were meeting in better circumstances. I'm Nick Daniels.'

Nick Daniels extended his hand to me. His grasp was firm and strong and he smiled while he shook my hand. It was a smile that emanated from his whole face and warm, hazel eyes bore into my soul. He was handsome in a rugged, youthful way, yet still managed to look experienced. His hair was on the darker side of fair, short on the back and sides, with a heavy fringe that he pushed back from his forehead as he spoke. God, he was gorgeous. I dragged my eyes from his.

Focus Ally, now is not the time to drool over this guy.

'Please, call me Ally. What's happened? Something more than a rape has happened tonight, hasn't it? I can tell from the increased police presence and . . . well, it feels different.'

'Yes, Ally, you're right. I'll walk you through what's happened, but under no circumstances are these details to go any further, okay?'

'Of course.'

'Guys, can you give me five minutes to bring Ms Can . . . Ally, up to speed, and then we'll regroup to go over our next steps? Thanks. Jake, can you speak with the ex-husband? He'll be anxious to get an update on her condition.'

Nick managed to clear the room of the badges including Detective Inspector Jake De Stefano, who looked a little disgruntled at having to leave. It had been rumoured throughout town that Jake had expected to get promoted until the gorgeous Nick appeared on the scene and kyboshed his plans. I smiled and looked away. The last thing I needed was for Jake De Stefano to get uppity if he thought I was being smug at getting the DCI's attention all to myself.

'Ally, we would've called you earlier but the victim has just come out of surgery. She's recovering now, still drowsy, but we want you there when she wakes.'

'Surgery? I don't understand. How severe was the rape?'

'She was raped, Ally, but she was also stabbed. There are details that are unclear at present, and we are hoping Mrs Garby can tell us what happened.'

'I'm sorry . . . What? Who?' My mouth fell open and I silently gasped like a fish dragged out of water. 'Dr Gill Garby? That's the victim?'

'I'm sorry. Didn't Michelle tell you? You know Dr Garby, right?'

I nodded. Was I going to be able to deal professionally with this? Sure, we spoke about client referrals regularly, but we'd also had the odd catch up over a glass of wine or coffee. She was my friend. I couldn't believe that she was the victim.

'She was attacked coming out of the gym last

night. The perp raped and stabbed her. It looked like she was able to use her mobile to call for help before she fell unconscious. And she's sustained a blow to her head.'

'Oh God, poor Gill. Where was she stabbed?'

'The pelvic area. She lost a lot of blood, and they had to do a hysterectomy – there was just too much damage. She's been in surgery then recovery since she was brought in.'

I put my face in my hands. Why would anyone do this? Why?

'Are you okay, Ally? Look, I called you for several reasons. They said you were the best counsellor and this is a situation that is going to need someone that can handle the circumstances . . . as gruesome as they are. Even though you know Dr Garby, she needs someone she can trust at this time. We need the facts, Ally.'

'Of course. I want to help. I just didn't expect it to be someone I know quite well.'

'Do you know of anyone that may have wanted to hurt her?'

'You think someone chose her specifically? I . . . I thought this was just a random attack. Are you suggesting this was something else?'

'No, not at all. Just covering all the bases here. Let's go see if she's awake, eh?'

Inspector Gorgeous put his hand on my arm to escort me to the recovery room to see Gill. Had the situation not been so bloody horrific I might have lapped up his attention, but not now. I also guessed there was something else that he knew and wasn't telling me, or perhaps it was just the unanswered questions.

Gill looked like crap. Attempts had been made to clean her up but there was caked blood around her hairline, she was deathly pale with black circles around her eyes and her lips looked dry from the oxygen mask she had on. She was still drowsy but her eyes flickered with recognition when I entered the room.

'Gill . . . I'm so sorry . . .'

Gill shook her head, but tears collected in the corner of her eyes before sliding down her cheeks. I knew the police would want some details as soon as possible. I wanted to hold her hand, but hesitated.

'Can I touch her? Has she had samples taken?' Nick was standing close by, but giving me space to connect to Gill. He nodded without speaking, indicating that forensic samples had been collected, as they did whenever someone had been raped, or worse, murdered. I picked her hand up and held it in mine hoping that I could pass some of my strength through my fingertips. Hers felt cold, almost lifeless.

'Gill, who did this to you? Did you see them?'

She tried to part her lips to answer, but they were stuck together, so I removed her oxygen mask and rubbed her lips with the gauze covered ice chips placed by her bedside.

'H– head covered . . . didn't s . . . see. Kn . . . knocked me out . . . don't remember . . .'

'But you managed to call for help Gill – on your mobile.' I tried to prompt her, to remind her.

'Th . . . that wasn't me. I didn't call. Has anyone called my husband, Steven? My ex actually, but we're still close. P . . . please, he needs to know where I am.' She looked anxiously between Nick and me.

'He knows, Gill,' Nick answered. 'He's in the waiting room with DI De Stefano. He'll come and see you shortly. He's worried, but he knows what's happened.'

'I thought you said she'd called for help?' My

eyes looked to Nick and he came forward to the bed. 'Gill, this is Detective Chief Inspector Nick Daniels, he's going to find out who did this to you.'

Gill nodded and smiled weakly to acknowledge him.

'Gill, I'm sorry to be asking you these questions now. I'm sorry for what you've been through, but it's important to get as much information as possible. You said you had something over your head?' Gill nodded to his question. 'Can you tell us more? Do you remember what happened next?'

'No, he . . . he put something over my head. He was behind me and I can't remember what happened.' Then she put a hand up to her neck as if recalling something. There was a reddish-blue line around her neck.

'My neck. I think he was strangling me with a cord or something. I . . . I don't know. I woke up, there was something stuffed in my mouth, and my hands . . . they were tied behind me and he was . . .' Gill choked back her sobs as she recalled the scene.

God, how do you recover from this trauma?

'Th . . . then the pain. He laughed but the pain was so bad, I think I passed out then.'

'You're doing well, Gill. We know this is hard but everything you tell us is one step closer to helping us find this bastard. Did he say anything? Did you recognise his voice?'

'I . . . I don't think so.' She shook her head, looking frustrated.

'You didn't make the call for help? Maybe you can't remember?' Nick probed gently. But she shook her head in answer.

'So *he* called?' I searched the inspector's eyes for answers.

'Someone dialled for help; they didn't speak.

We just thought she must have passed out.' Nick patted Gill's hand and left the room with more questions than we'd had before she woke up.

***

'Jeez. You look like shit.' Ping went Jinny's swear app.

'Good morning to you, too' Ally snorted in response. 'I've been up since half four this morning. It's not been a good day so far.' She pulled out a chair at her favourite table. The café had just opened and was thankfully quiet, except for the staff preparing food for the day's customers.

'Does this have anything to do with what was on the news this morning? The radio said that the road leading up to the gym was closed and the police were doing an investigation. That was all they said, though. There wasn't a rape, was there?'

Ally wasn't really in the mood to answer any of Jinny's questions, but she badly needed breakfast, or at least a coffee, and not that God awful, black gloop at the centre, before going into work.

'Ssh. Yes. There was a rape. I can't really talk about it. There's an investigation . . .'

'I'm not going to say anything, Ally. Is she, whoever it was, okay?' Jinny's eyes pleaded with Ally for information.

'Jinny, it's horrible. Look, I can't say much, but I want you to be safe. This was a bit too close to home.'

'What are you on about, Ally? What's happened?' Jinny lowered her voice, pulled out the chair next to her sister, sat down and leaned in closer.

'It was Gill, Gill Garby. She was fucking raped and stabbed. They don't know who did it, Jinny. She nearly died.' Ally blabbed it all out. It was her sister, she thought. They told each other everything and

40

anyway, who was going to counsel the counsellor when the shit piled up so high it threatened to collapse and bury her underneath it all?

Jinny sat back in her chair, stunned. 'Fuck! And I thought my life was shit. I was gonna tell you that me and Fiona are taking a break.'

'Aw, that is shit Jinny. I'm sorry.'

'I've moved back here, to the flat.'

'Are you okay? D' you want to stay at mine? The company would be good.'

And safe.

'Nah. I need some space to think, y' know?'

'Okay. Maybe it'll be good for you and Fiona; time to think about what's best. You know where I am if you need me.' Ally put her hand on Jinny's.

When Roz appeared from the kitchen with two freshly prepared breakfasts, the sisters soon sat back and pushed their plates away. Food just didn't seem so appealing now.

***

Jinny

After hearing customers in the café talk about nothing but the rape all morning, I thought it would be better to go and pack my stuff up at Fiona's during daylight hours and not have to drive back down that quiet country road by myself at night. It also meant I didn't have to see Fiona if she was at the office. But her car was in the drive. Fuck. Well, I wasn't going to turn back now. I needed my clothes and my toiletries; luckily just about everything else I owned was digital: books, music, films.

I parked behind Fiona's car and let myself in the kitchen door. Fi wasn't about the bottom of the

41

house as I gathered up my Garmin, Kindle, chargers, sunglasses, my quirky word-a-day calendar. I grabbed my backpack from the hall cupboard and went upstairs. The bedroom door was closed. It wasn't like Fi to be still in bed this late unless she was sick. I felt guilty. Had I made her ill with all my nonsense? Damn. Maybe we should just kiss and make up. Or make out. I opened the door and Fi was in bed, on top of fucking Kevin. Literally fucking Kevin. He looked at me and gasped as Fi turned around, her eyes opening wide. She jumped off him letting his dick whip back with a splat. Christ, his dick was huge. I don't think I'd ever seen a dick that big unless it was fucking Day-Glo pink and silicon.

'Fuck,' Kev said, my phone responding to his profanity and I was angry at that liberty.

I just looked at Fi. Her swollen mouth gaping open as she watched me methodically and calmly go around the room emptying my stuff into my backpack. Kev at least had the courtesy of covering his humungous appendage. Fucking humungous!

It didn't take long to remove my presence from her room, her life. I don't know why I was so calm. It was like my intuition was revelling in being right. They were so still and silent, all I could hear was their heavy breathing and the swishing of drawers opening and closing as I went through each one. Would she look at the empty spaces and miss me or had she already moved on? Would Kevin's enormous pants soon be filling the void? I suppose he was quite good-looking, if you were into men, which I didn't think Fi was. The sheen of sweat glistened on his dark coffee-coloured skin, emphasising his amazing muscular physique. Short, black hair, a good definition of stubble, high cheekbones, full lips; he had more muscle than brains, especially between the legs.

Why him? What was the attraction – apart from the obvious – to a man, for fuck's sake? I stuffed the last of my gear into my bag and took in a deep breath; it wasn't pleasant, a citrus aftershave, sweat and a heady maleness I wasn't used to. I looked Fi in the eye. She tried to look away but I held her gaze.

'I guess this is it,' she said. It wasn't much of a question, more a statement of the current situation.

'You can email me about the client division. I trust you'll be fair.'

She just nodded.

'Right.' I looked at her. It was a long look to underline the fact that this *was* it, that I was leaving, but her eyes broke away from mine.

I piled my belongings into the car and had one last look at the house. The sun was high behind it, outlining the front and shading the façade. It looked dull and sad in that light. I wouldn't miss it. I turned the car and headed back to my bright, spacious courtyard flat behind the café, relieved that I'd never bothered renting it out. It was always a handy haven for friends to stay in when they came to visit, or staff to relax in if they worked double shifts. It had even been the occasional refuge for broken relationships - including mine now. It always felt like home to me, especially today.

The whole café-flat package had belonged to my first girlfriend, Beth. We'd met at university and her mother had owned the café back then. When her mother got diagnosed with bloody breast cancer and needed some help while going through the rigors of chemotherapy, Beth quit her degree to look after her. I commuted between here and the uni for a year, until I finished my degree, and then I moved in. I worked remotely for a small data mining company so I could help out in the café. Her mum died only after a couple of months of me being there. Beth and I cemented our relationship in a civil partnership. Then she discovered a fucking lump too. Well, I did, actually. I found it when we were having a good old romp. Turned out it had already spread. We did get a good couple of years together before I lost her. We hadn't even made love in the last year or so as she just didn't have the energy but I didn't care. I wanted to be with her, to look after her. She stayed upbeat while she was getting treatment for advanced cancer, and then it wasn't even the fucking cancer but some bloody candida infection that got her in the end. An opportunistic infection, the doctors called it. I was distraught.

She'd left me the café, the flat, her savings, everything. I kept on working remotely at the café to take my mind off not having her. Then, about a year after she died, I met Fi at a computer software convention. We hit it off, especially when she said she lived only ten miles away. And now I'm back to where I started. And somehow it felt right as I drove into my little courtyard, the sun shining on my windows and doors welcoming me home. Home. It was 5.15 p.m. I texted Ally.

Can you come to café for dinner?

Sure. Be there in an hour or so. Just about to have last session today.

C U soon. Xx

Good. That gave me enough time to unpack and settle back in.

***

Ally

'God dammit.'

'What's up?' Sharon queried, coming into the small kitchen area to find me with my arm in the fridge, holding an empty carton.

'There's no soya milk left. It was a full carton two days ago.' I straightened up, shaking the offending carton to prove my point.

'Er, sorry.'

'What the hell, Sharon? Since when did you start taking soya milk? You usually drink hormone-laden, bovine secretions.'

'I know. I ran out, started using soya and guess I got kinda used to it. I'll nip out and get more – by the way, your last appointment is waiting for you in the counselling room.' She turned on the heel of her bright orange, garish stilettos and left, leaving the scent of her overpowering perfume behind her.

'Mind get organic,' I shouted to her retreating figure. Annoyed that I had no soya milk, I left the kitchen to counsel my last client for the day.

'Charley, how are you?'

Charlotte Proctor, John, the minister's sister – or Charley, as she preferred to be called – looked small, petite and vulnerable among the cushions of the sofa, but her appearance was a stark contrast to the personality I had grown to know and like in the year since we started her counselling sessions. She had come a long way. Just nineteen when she was raped, she never spoke much about the particulars, most of it had been repressed by her subconscious mind, but from what she did say I'd learned it had been brutal, leaving her traumatised mentally,

45

emotionally and physically.

Previous sessions had gained her history. At seventeen, Charley had left home to start nurse training in London. Almost half way through her father had a stroke, and her mother demanded she came home to help. She really didn't want to even though she felt guilty – I remember the happiness on her face when she described London life: her friends, living the scene. There was joy on her face, her blue eyes sparkling, when she told me she had realised she was gay and how accepted and supported she'd felt by her friends. The session where she described coming out to her parents was not a good day, though. We'd used regression therapy; there were gaps in her memory, but Charley did remember that day . . .

'I was scared. My heart was racing, but I hated the lie. Why should I feel ashamed? They shoved their outdated morals down our throats all our lives,' she'd said. 'I'd had enough. And with Dad now not able to talk and spout forth his evangelical beliefs, I decided to tell my mum. I honestly thought she'd be sympathetic. I don't know why I thought it would be a good idea to tell her as we were tending to my dad, maybe I was feeling rebellious. Actually, I think I wanted him to suffer.'

When Charley had lapsed into silence, I prompted her. 'What did she say when you told her? Remember, you are in a safe environment now. You are just an observer. Can you tell me what happened?'

Charley's eyes moved rapidly behind her closed lids. Her cheeks were slightly flushed and she frowned as she recalled the events. 'She just looked at my dad, and before I knew it, his good hand grabbed my hair and he held me down while my mother came

46

around to my side of the bed and slapped and slapped my face, bursting my nose. There was blood everywhere. I managed to shove her backwards to give me time to prise my father's hand open . . .' Again she paused, her breathing rapid.

'Nice deep breath in, Charley. Remember, you are just watching, observing.' I gave her a moment as I watched her breathing slow again. 'What happened next?'

'She lay there on the floor, sitting up against the wall, grasping her chest and staring at me. I knew she was going into cardiac arrest, but for all my training I just stood and watched as she lapsed into unconsciousness. At that point my training kicked in and I tried to resuscitate her, but it was too late. Maybe if I'd acted sooner . . .'

'How do you feel about that, Charley?'

'I was glad. I know that sounds awful, but I felt for the first time in my life that I was free to be me. Truly free.'

'What about your father? How did you feel about him?'

'I hated him. I spat in his face after she died. I refused to look after him. John had been away, but came right home and stepped in. Said he understood. Dad died two days later. And I was so relieved. I realised then that I'd never loved my parents, and they never really loved me. They spent all their lives trying to shape me and John into what they wanted us to be, but they didn't really show us love.'

'Is that all you remember from that time, Charley?'

She had been silent, a tear leaking from her eye and streaking slowly into a darker trail in her blonde hair. Her voice was almost a whisper when she replied. 'No. I remember it was the time I lost my virginity, to a man – when I was raped, I mean. He took that from me. It wasn't his to take. Not for any man to take. But he did. I still can't see everything that happened that night. Just bits and pieces, like a puzzle with lost parts. The doctors said he'd raped me and he'd also used a hairbrush. My hairbrush. It was brutal they said. I've blocked it out. Sometimes I try to remember, but other times, I still don't want to.' She looked away from me as she spoke, maybe turning away from the humiliating and intimate details that no woman should have to experience.

'You don't need to remember, Charley. If you do, it will come back when you are ready. How did you cope after it? Can you talk about that?' I urged gently.

'John helped. He consoled me. Let me talk about everything, about how I felt about mum and dad. He felt guilty he was out of the house the night it happened. The police said I'd called them, but I don't remember. The phone beside my bed was off the hook and they found me beaten and bloody. The police never found the intruder, and I couldn't help as I didn't remember what happened.'

Again, she'd lapsed into silence. Another tear rolled in the trail of the last. I didn't say anything; she'd never revealed any of this before in ordinary sessions. Then she started to speak again. 'John encouraged me to go back to nursing. He was right. I did. It helped me put it behind me. John also left to do a theology degree. It was the best thing for both of us.' She smiled at that.

I knew it was as much as we'd get from her that session; it was the most informative we'd had. And from then until now we'd worked together without the need for regression again. Charley had qualified as a nurse a couple of years later and stayed in

London, working long, hard hours, caring for everyone else except herself, and trying to forget. And so the cracks appeared, she told me, slowly at first, and she managed them with some self-loathing and a great deal of self-mutilation. Cutting eased the pain, until one cut too deep, one Charley never wanted to recover from. After the failed suicide attempt, John went to London and helped her to recover; his degree in theology complete, he'd gained an understanding into people's mental woes, being minister and counsellor. He'd been minister in several towns by then, but chose to come home and settle again in Covenston. He convinced Charley to come with him, to use their empty family home, The Old Manse, as a shelter for women, asking her to manage it. She didn't want to come back to that place, but her brother had been so supportive she didn't want to let him down either. She also knew it would be a good way to face her inner demons head on.

And that's where we were now. After a year of counselling, and a year of Charley being back in Covenston, we were having one final session.

'I'm ready, Ally,' she announced.

'What for, Charley?'

'Living. It's been too long,' she beamed as she spoke.

'I'm so glad, Charley. You've been so resilient, strong. Even if you haven't been able to always see it, I have, and I knew this day would come.'

Was she truly ready though? Maybe I should encourage her to keep seeing me for longer?

'I've had good support. John's been great and then there's you, too. I've also joined a new group, a friendship type of group that's been really supportive too.' Charley paused. Her body language and eye position indicated to me that she was thinking about

49

this new group. I knew if she wanted to tell me more she would, but for now I was confident her support network was solid enough for her to let our sessions drop.

'You've come a long way. When you started coming here you were cutting yourself most days.'

'It's been so long since I felt the need to do that. Helping other women has helped me. Made my pain less.'

'We never managed to uncover the details of the man that raped you, Charley, even in our regression sessions. How do you feel about that now? Does it bother you that there're still gaps in your memory?' I questioned, worried that she may need more support in the future when or if her memories return.

'It did bother me. But I guess I'll remember when the time is right. You said the memories might come back when I feel safe enough to remember.'

'It's different for everyone. Do you feel safe enough – yet?'

'Erm, I'm not sure. But how long can I hold off living my life until I do? I might never feel safe enough. And people get hurt all the time. By family, by strangers . . . I just want a life of my own, maybe a relationship.' Charley moved excitedly in her seat. 'I've thrown myself into the work at the refuge for so long, that I didn't realise I was deliberately making excuses not to move on – not to get involved with anyone. And John always helped in that respect, keeping me busy, afraid I'd relapse into depression, but I'm good now. I am, Ally.' Charley looked at me and I could see the sincerity of her words. I questioned further, just to be sure.

'I'm glad you want to start enjoying life but I'm worried you might want a relationship to give you that feeling of safety, instead of trusting yourself.'

'I'll be careful. And if I need help I'll reach out. I promise. I've been alone too long. Resisting the need to find out what it's like to be with a woman. It's all I've been thinking about. I'm so ready.'

'Does this signal the end of our sessions, Charley?' I knew I really had to let her go. She just seemed so young and vulnerable. I felt like a mother not wanting to let their child go off into the big, bad world.

Charley looked down, thinking silently, searching her inner resources. Was she able to let go of our sessions? She lifted her chin, defiantly and smiled. 'Yes, yes it does.'

With Charley gone, and appointments finished, I grabbed my coat and bag. Sharon had already left. She'd left a note on the fridge:

New carton of soya milk for you m'lady, apologies for guzzling the last one but I'm a converted woman, so you can't be too hard on me. See you tomorrow. Xx

I laughed at the note and closed up the centre for the night, before strolling slowly along the street-lit pavement. The working day had ended positively with Charley feeling well enough to end her counselling. That didn't happen too often so I was going to make the most of the good feeling before I met up with Jinny for our dinner date at the café. Heartbreak and tears would no doubt be on tonight's menu.

***

Jinny was sitting at their table by the time Ally

arrived, slightly later than she'd said. Jinny waved to Linda who nodded and went into the kitchen to get their order.

'You get my usual?' Ally asked, knowing fine she had.

Jinny just raised an eyebrow at her. 'So how's it going at work?' she asked, wanting to delay having to tell Ally about her shocking day until their food was on the table and they had privacy to talk.

'Today ended on a good note. One of the patients I've had for a year felt it was time to end our sessions. I'm so pleased for her. I knew she had reached that point a few weeks ago, but I think she was just afraid to let go of the crutch just yet. But she did it today, and I'm just elated.'

Linda came over with the tray, and balancing it on the edge of their table she placed the tofish, peas and chips under each of them, along with a couple of glasses of home-made lemonade. 'Enjoy,' she smiled and left them to it.

The smoked tofu steamed a hot trail right into Jinny's nostrils. She loved this dish. The crispy batter made with secret beer recipe was a bestseller at the café, and the meal was one of Ally and Jinny's once-a-week favourite treats. Ally was already tucking into her meal, while Jinny covered hers in tomato ketchup.

'So how was your day?' Ally asked mainly without consonants, as her mouth was full.

'You know how you said I was being paranoid about Fi?'

'Ah-huh...'

'Well, I wasn't. I fucking caught her in bed with a well-endowed Kevin.'

'Shit!' Ally spat out some of her meal as she swore. Both their phones vibrated twice on the table.

'Damn.' They pinged again. Ally rolled her eyes. 'How did you catch them? Surely they weren't doing it at the office?'

Jinny swallowed her lump in her throat with a mouthful of peas. She wasn't going to cry over this. She was just feeling sorry for herself, because in reality, she probably hadn't really been happy with Fiona for a while now. 'I went home to get my things and found them at it in our bed. Our fucking bed.' Jinny still couldn't get the picture of Kevin's enormous penis out her head. She'd chucked out her black dildo when she unpacked. 'To be honest, I'm relieved I was right. And I wasn't going bloody crazy.'

'I'm so sorry that happened. I thought you two were good together. I was worried about you when Beth died. I was happy to see you get together with Fiona. Are you sure you're okay?'

'I am, Ally. I really am. In fact, I'm sure in a couple of days I'll look back on it and bloody laugh. I wish you could've seen his dick, Al. He could make a fortune in the porn industry.'

Ally almost choked on her dinner, and sipped on her lemonade to clear her throat. 'Bitch. I think my imagination is doing a pretty good job of visualising it.'

'Yeah, it's true what they say, you know. Be careful what you wish for.'

'What do you mean? You were being paranoid, Jinny. You didn't wish for it. You didn't wish to break up with Fiona.'

Jinny felt her face flush when she remembered her outdoor, unholy hour, naked exploits.

Ally was watching her closely. You couldn't hide much from a psychologist. 'What? Tell me. Why do you think you've brought this on yourself? Hmm?'

Jinny didn't know where to start. She hadn't

intended to tell Ally for fear of ridicule. But fuck it, she might as well give her a laugh. 'I . . . eh . . . I tried a spell.'

'What d'you mean you tried a spell? How? What did you do?'

'Well, I'd read online about manifesting your desires, so I googled it some more and found all these YouTube vids on making spells to manifest what you want.'

'For fuck's sake.' Their phones vibrated. 'I've heard it all now. What the he–' Ally looked at their phones, 'heck did you do?' She smiled coyly.

'To cut a long story short, I wrote my desire, which was to get Kevin out of my fucking life, on a piece of paper and made a spell, like a rhyme, about what I wanted. I stripped naked–'

'What? Are you mad?'

'It was part of the spell. Naked under the full moon. Anyway, I chanted my spell, burned it and hoped for the best.'

'So you successfully got rid of Kevin, and Fiona too . . .'

'See! Be careful what you wish for. It said that in everything I watched. I obviously fucked up.'

Ally switched her phone off. Jinny couldn't stop herself swearing, it's why she'd invented the app, to try and curb her nasty habit, so she left hers on. She might as well pay for her foul language. 'You're not saying anything? You're not going to tell me I was an idiot?'

'You are. But it's just strange. That's the second time this week I've heard of witchcraft.'

'No way! Who? What?'

'Just someone I know suggested I join their *coven*.' Ally used finger quotes. 'Then they tried to lessen my disbelief by telling me it was more of a healing group. Look, I've got the leaflet somewhere.' Ally finished her last forkful, shoved her plate away and pulled her bag in front of her to rummage. She pulled out a wrinkled leaflet with a few grease stains on it and handed it to Jinny. 'Sorry, it was beside my biscuits.'

Jinny lifted it gingerly, pulling it straight with the tips of her fingers. 'The Towers Coven. Practising an Eclectic form of Wicca to create wholeness and abundance. Look, it says they meet every Saturday evening. Tomorrow.' Jinny looked at Ally questioningly.

'Oh, no. Not a good idea.' Ally shook her head, looking around her, hoping no one saw Jinny lift the garish leaflet. The silver pentagram on a purple background was screaming cult group insanity. 'Not me. You go, if you want. Be better than dancing around the garden bollock-naked. Leave me out of this.'

'Oh come on. We could go for a laugh. Look, it says they discuss how they can help the community, healing workshops and help manifest your dreams. That sounds okay.'

'Nope. Nope. Nope. You'll not convince me to go.'

'It's up at the Towers. Not a lane I want to troop up myself after that rape. I'll not bother.' Ally sighed. Jinny knew she was guilt-tripping her. 'You shouldn't have told me about them. Then I wouldn't be missing out.' Ally sighed again. Jinny waited. She knew it was coming. She put on her really sad face. Let her eyes water a little. Swallowed a bit and blinked. Ally's cheeks were tightening.

Here it's coming. Maybe look away, blinking, a sniff too.

'Oh fuck. Alright. But just to let you see what it's

55

like and make friends so you can go with them.' Jinny beamed at her. 'Bitch, you knew you could change my mind.'

'I knew you wouldn't want me going up that lane in the dark alone after what's happened. So yeah.'

'I must admit, I'm looking over my shoulder all the time. We're just a tight-knit community. We're not used to this kind of crime.'

'I know. It's shaken everyone up. That's been the buzz all day here.'

Linda came and gathered up their empty plates. 'You want your dessert just now?'

Jinny looked at Ally. Her smile said it all; the chocolate cake was to die for and on Friday evenings they always had cake. 'Yep. Bring it out. We'll be rolling home tonight.'

'At least you've not far to roll.' Ally pointed her dessert spoon at her.

'You can crash here if you want. I've a nice Shiraz in the flat.'

Ally looked pensive. Jinny knew she was thinking about the drive back to her own place in the dark, a rapist on the loose.

'Okay. Let's eat cake, then get pished. You can tell me more about Kevin's dick. I've not had any in a while.'

CHAPTER FIVE

What the hell was she thinking, agreeing to go to that witchy thing tonight? Ally wondered as she tidied her hair and reapplied her lipstick. She didn't like anything with a culty feel to it and believed those types of groups tended to prey on the most vulnerable of people. Who knew? Maybe she'd really enjoy it, but to top it off, the night was miserable, dark, wet and windy. Ally imagined naked witches dancing around a fire and shivered.

There's no way I'll be getting up to any naked shenanigans in this weather, or for any reason.

Hearing Jinny toot her horn outside, she pulled on her warmest padded coat and tried to put on a pleasant face to hide the foreboding feeling growing in her.

'Excited?' Jinny asked as she opened the door of the car.

'Not really,' answered Ally as truthfully as she could. 'I'm really only going for you, remember.'

'I know, but it might be good. I'm looking forward to it. It's different, and I could do with something to take my mind off everything that's going on just now.'

'Have you heard from Fiona?'

'She sent me an email, asking to meet next week at some point, to settle any leftover business stuff. I haven't got back to her. I can't face her yet. She can just wait until I'm bloody ready.'

They turned off the main road on the outskirts of town, navigating the many potholes on a long, lumpy driveway, as they made their way up to the not yet visible property. The driveway would be beautiful in a few months, with the tunnel of cherry and apple blossom trees in full bloom, but tonight was eerie; bare trees whipping about in the wind created jagged shadows on the road. At the end of the drive lay an impressive mid-nineteenth century Gothic manse, complete with turrets and arched windows. The Towers sure looked impressive.

Ally felt as if she was about to star in her own cringe-worthy, horror movie. 'Oh God, let's get in before I change my mind.'

'It certainly looks the part,' admitted an excited Jinny. She pushed the round doorbell and they waited silently until Amira threw open the door and beamed a smile at them both.

'Ally, Jinny. I'm so glad you came. Debbie said she'd asked you along.'

They smiled back apprehensively as Amira welcomed them into the large hallway. Ally gave her the once over, thinking that their hostess looked like she'd assumed the role of high priestess in a fitted black velvety long dress, which tapered out at her feet and wrists.

Extending her arm, Amira indicated that they follow her into the large lounge off the main hallway. The room was dimly lit with candles placed on sideboards and on top of the enormous fireplace. That was the main feature of the room, its dancing flames creating a warm glow over the well-worn armchairs and sofa around it. At one end of the room, the furniture had been pushed back to leave a large open space where a small group of people sat on scattered cushions on a threadbare rug. They all looked up inquisitively and the atmosphere felt awkward as the newcomers approached the circle.

'Everyone, it's Jinny and Ally. Oh ladies, let me introduce you to our little group. I'm sure you know most of us, anyway. You both know my darling, hubby, Nasir; then there's Debbie, of course; Simon, Robert, Ayesha, Julia and Charley. Please take a seat – we were just about to begin.' Amira crossed her legs on a purple cushion.

As she and Jinny tried to blend in on their own cushions, Ally glanced round the group. 'Shit, I know someone else here,' she whispered to Jinny, catching the surprised look from Charley as Ally smiled quickly and looked away. 'I knew this wasn't a good idea. Meeting clients at social events when you know their most intimate details was not included in any plan,' Ally hissed under her breath. Jinny looked apologetic but they both knew it was too late to do anything about it.

The group was of mixed ages; Amira and Nasir Bamra, the eldest, in their late sixties. Everyone else looked closer to Jinny and Ally in age, except for Ayesha, who was an attractive South African girl in her late teens. They all looked friendly, especially Amira and Nasir who had become well-known in the community for their lavish, extravagant parties since they had moved into The Towers and renovated it from its former, crumbling self.

'This week,' Amira started, looking around the members, 'we're going to start with a meditation, to ease the energy in the room and try to bring the focus to create a positive, healing environment.'

'Especially because of recent events in the community.' Nasir didn't need to explain further, everyone knew he was referring to the brutal assault on Gill and the ongoing investigation.

'So, if everyone could close their eyes and focus on their breathing...'

What brought these people to this group? Ally wondered as she peeped through half-closed eyes around the circle. She understood why Charley was there. This type of gathering could help to channel her fears, improve her self-esteem and help to give her some control, instead of her previous powerlessness. As for the rest of them, who knew what skeletons lay in their closets – most people had one or two. Ally's eyes took in each person in turn, imagining their personal details, until she locked gazes with Simon. He narrowed his dark eyes as he looked back, then smirked as if he could read her thoughts. Feeling transparent and uncomfortable, Ally closed her eyes in an attempt to block him out. Simon was tall and wiry with shoulder-length dark grey hair, which he had tied back into a pony tail, and an unruly, dark greying beard. Ally pictured food getting tangled in it as he ate.

Urgh.

She hated thinking badly of someone she didn't know, but he creeped her out. She was trying desperately to resist the urge to open her eyes to see if he was still leering when Amira ended the meditation and offered refreshments in the kitchen diner.

'What do you think so far?' Debbie asked as Ally was getting some fruit juice.

'Hmm, yeah. It's uh, fine. How's Anne?'

'She's okay. But she's moved back to The

Gables. I tried to get her to see sense but . . .'

'At the end of the day it's Anne's choice. She's an adult. All we can do is be there, support her and keep an eye on her. I'll pop in to see her next week.'

'Ally, did you enjoy the first half of our evening, the meditation?' Nasir interrupted.

'Yes, thanks Nasir, it was very calming. Erm . . . I was trying to find out a wee bit more about witchcraft. Y' know, what kind is it? What does this coven do?'

'Ah, of course you must have lots of questions. Our coven practises an Eclectic form of Wicca. As practitioners we each bring our own style and beliefs. Amira and I used to practise Gardnerian Wicca, but over the years and our interaction with various covens and witches, we embraced a more Eclectic style.'

'I don't know all the different types, I've only read a small amount about it. Gardnerian, that's based on the teachings from Gerald Gardner, the so-called father of Wicca, right?'

'Yes, that's right. He's thought to be the man that revived witchcraft in the modern world. But witchcraft has been around for thousands of years. What is witchcraft anyway? It's such a confusing term. Most cultures have someone that was deemed to be a practitioner of magic, a witch doctor, a healer, midwives. They tried to understand nature, plants, the changing seasons, the cycle of life, even astronomy. They used energy, potions and rituals to heal the sick. Some say they were the original doctors. Modern religion and medicine made us forget our Wiccan pasts. We now rely on doctors to heal our bodies and ministers to guide us in our spiritual beliefs. But, as witches we believe that we can heal ourselves and that our spiritual and physical health are not separate entities.'

'So healing the body and mind through spells; how does that work?' Ally was genuinely interested. After all, she practiced clinical hypnosis and relaxation techniques and witnessed people recover from various illnesses when they let go of the stresses and anxiety plaguing their lives. But magic and spells seemed a step too far down the rabbit hole.

'Our minds are powerful tools, Ally. You know about the placebo effect?' As he spoke, a black cat with a white patch on its chest appeared from underneath the table and began weaving itself through Nasir's legs. It meowed loudly for attention, and so he picked it up, cradling it in his arms. The cat purred contentedly, rubbing its head against Nasir's chin, claiming ownership with its scent.

'Aw, I love cats. So independent, yet loving.' Ally made small cooing noises as she stroked the cat's chin. 'What's its name?'

'This is Dumbledore, our familiar. I think he owns us rather than the opposite.'

'Ha, ha. Going by how happy and smug he looks just now, I think you are right.'

'Okay, everyone. It's time to get on. Let's move back to the circle, please.' Amira brought everyone's conversations to an abrupt halt. Ally looked around for Jinny, who was engrossed in a conversation with Charley; she wondered if Charley had told her that she and Ally knew each other.

'Ally, I was hoping to get a chat with you but Nasir kept you all to himself.'

Ally felt Simon's hand catch her arm and then slide around her waist as they walked towards the lounge. She didn't like it. She didn't know the man and his eyes were crawling over her breasts as he spoke. She felt invaded. She caught Jinny's eye and silently beseeched her sister to help. She could see Jinny was enjoying her conversation with Charley, but as Ally watched, Jinny excused herself and headed over.

'Ally, could you help me fix the zip on my jeans, please? Ha, women's problems, eh Simon?' Jinny redirected Ally to the downstairs toilet near the entrance to the lounge.

'Are you okay? I saw you lurch away from Mr Leechy,' Jinny asked as she locked the toilet door behind.

'Was I that obvious? He creeps me out, and I hate it when men think they can put their hands onto a woman without their permission.'

'I know. That makes me bloody mad, too. Charley's nice. We were chatting a while.'

'Yeah, I noticed. Look Jin, I think–'

A sharp rap at the bathroom stalled the conversation. 'Ally, Jinny, are you in there? We're about to start.'

'I think that was Debbie. We'd better get out there.' Jinny took an eyeliner pencil out of her pocket and quickly darkened the lines around her eyes, making her brown eyes stand out even more. She took a last look in the mirror and unlocked the door.

Ally was relieved; she wasn't sure what to say anyway to Jinny about Charley. She certainly wasn't about to break client confidentiality and both women were responsible adults – yet she felt protective over both of them.

'Ladies, please come, stand around the circle.' Amira beckoned to them, the last to return. Everyone had linked hands, and Robert reached his out to Jinny as the sisters joined the group.

'We are about to draw our magic circle, which will protect, guide and strengthen our magic. Each week we perform a ritual or a healing. We prefer to do something that will benefit the community in some way. Simon has asked us to perform a ritual this week to find his neighbour's dog, which went missing on Thursday. He has placed a picture of the dog on our altar to help us focus our thoughts. The dog's name is Benji.'

Jinny and Ally looked over their shoulders at a picture of a scruffy-looking border terrier on a temporary altar surrounded by candles, a pentagram and an athame – the ceremonial knife; Ally had looked it up earlier.

Nasir took to the centre of the circle, closing his eyes, and spun round three times. 'I ask that the God and Goddess bless this circle. So that we may be free, and protected within this space. So mote it be.' He moved around the circle, placing different coloured candles at various points while continuing to ask for protection for the circle. Once done, he looked to the rest of the circle and asked them to join him in a further incantation.

'God and Goddess, Guardian Angels, and Spiritual Guides please be present with us during this ritual. Bless this circle and keep us protected. No unwanted entities are welcome here. Only pure, divine beings are invited into this space. The circle is cast. So mote it be.'

Nasir went out of the circle and swapped places with Amira, who placed a brown candle in the middle of the circle and then lit it. Asking everyone to think of Benji and imagine the lost dog finding its way back to safety in Simon's arms. She then chanted another incantation three times, asking everyone to say the words to themselves as she spoke:

'Diana, Goddess of the Wild.

Keeper of dogs both fierce and mild.

Hold Benji safely in your arms.
And protect this pet from all harm.
Should the day come that he roams
Guide him to the path back home.
So Mote It Be.'

Amira then called an end to the ritual and said another protection prayer for the community, with a specific emphasis on Dr Garby's speedy recovery. Everyone nodded and mumbled the words together, each undoubtedly thinking about the horrific event and what it meant to their own feelings of safety and security. The circle then broke and hushed conversations started among various couples. Ally moved quickly across the room to Charley.

'Charley. I didn't expect to see you here. I hope me being here tonight wasn't a problem?'

'Ha. I was pretty surprised to see you, Ally, but it's fine. I've actually told most of the group the basics of my story, that I was raped, and they've been really supportive.'

'Oh . . . is this the group you mentioned in our last session? I never even thought to ask. Well, don't worry, I would never breach our confidentiality, and anyway, I'm only here for Jinny. She fancied coming along and asked me to keep her company. New faces, and all that. Actually, I'm going to try grab her to get out of here. Once she starts a conversation there's no telling when I'll get her home.' Ally laughed, relieved that Charley didn't mind her being there.

'Hey, I hope that's not me you're bitching about,' Jinny interrupted. She'd been dying to get back to Charley again after breaking away to rescue Ally.

'Me?' Ally asked. 'You know I never bitch, sister.'

Jinny raised both eyebrows so high and

wiggled them that Charley and Ally laughed, and she joined in.

'I was just saying to Ally,' Charley offered, 'that I was surprised to see her here.'

Jinny didn't want to assume this was Ally's patient, but it made sense. She wasn't sure what to say, so she was relieved when Charley explained.

'I used to go to Ally for therapy. But I didn't ever imagine this would be your scene, Ally . . .'

'I dragged her along, or rather I emotionally blackmailed her.' Jinny nudged her sister who gave her a smirk. 'But I'm hoping she enjoyed it. Did you, Al?'

'Let's just say I found it interesting enough to come again.'

'You're just curious to see if the spell works, aren't you?' Jinny turned to Charley, 'Ally is sceptical about this sort of thing.'

'So was I initially, to be honest,' Charley admitted, 'but I liked the idea of a safe group to find out about meditation and self-healing. And it has helped heaps, hasn't it, Ally?'

Jinny could see Ally looked uncomfortable about talking about her work, but the smile she gave Charley was warm and genuine.

'Well, you have made great progress, so yeah it must be helpful. I did enjoy the meditation part, and I am interested in Wiccan history. When we were young, Jinny and I used to raid the library for all kinds of paranormal books. You remember?' Ally turned to Jinny, laughing.

'I think I still have some of those books,' Jinny explained to Charley, keeping her involved. She was happy to see she looked interested. 'If we liked the book, we'd nag our parents to buy us it. I might just dig them out again. Although you can get all sorts of info now on the internet.'

'I'd love to see those books, Jinny.' Charley smiled at Jinny.

Well, if that's not a 'come on' I'm losing my mind.

'Sure, I'll dig them out. I'll try find them before we come back here next week.'

'That'd be great.' Charley beamed.

Jinny made a note to pump her sister for info on her on the way home. Or maybe . . .

'You need a run home, Charley?' Jinny asked hopefully.

'Aw thanks, that's nice of you. But it's okay. Ayesha lives beside me. So we take it in turns to drive.'

'Good,' Ally interjected. 'Best to travel in numbers, after what happened.'

Charley looked sad for a moment, then agreed. 'Absolutely. Everyone is feeling it. John was even talking about arranging some self-defence classes.'

'I think we'd both be interested in that.' Ally nudged Jinny and looked at her questioningly.

She needn't have worried there; Jinny was keen. She'd done Shukokai Karate in her teens to purple belt level and in her mind's eye she was sure she'd be kicking ass in no time at all. A bit like riding a bike, she mused. 'Yep, count me in.'

'Great. I'll remind him about getting it organised sooner rather than later.'

Ayesha sauntered over to their group, passing Charley her coat and bag. Jinny was disappointed they didn't have longer to chat. She repeated her promise to dig out those books just so she could have an excuse to talk to her again.

No sooner had Ally closed the car door, Jinny pounced; she'd drive slowly too.

'So do tell me that woman is gay. Please tell me

you thought she was flirting with me.' Without having to look at her, Jinny could feel Ally roll her eyes. The sigh gave it away too.

'She is, but before you get your hopes up, I need to warn you off her–' Jinny could see Ally's hand go up in her peripheral vision before she could verbally retaliate. 'For a while, anyway. One, you've just broken up with Fi and I don't want you hurting Charley with a rebound relationship–' Ally's hand went up again at Jinny's intake of breath. 'And two, and more importantly, I don't want you getting hurt entering into a relationship with Charley, who is very vulnerable, Jinny.'

'I have no intention of hurting her or me, Ally. I just felt there was a little spark there. Honestly, I felt drawn to her.'

'You said that about Fi.'

'Did bloody not!'

'Did! Anyway, I just want you to take it easy. I'm not saying don't go there. I'm just saying give yourself and Charley time.'

Jinny pulled up outside Ally's cottage and looked at her. She knew her sister was just concerned about her. She couldn't fault her on that, but Ally didn't understand that spark. And yes, she had felt a bit like that when she'd met Fiona, but that was just the novelty and excitement of the pursuit of a new relationship. But the frisson of excitement she felt tonight, talking to Charley, was like it had been with Beth. She'd never thought she'd ever feel that again – but now wasn't the time to tell Ally that, she didn't want to worry her any more than necessary. And Ally would worry.

'Okay. I won't rush into anything, I promise. But if Charley comes after me, I won't push her away, Al.'

Ally sighed. 'Look, just play it by ear. Give

yourself time to grieve for Fi and when you're sure you're over that, then consider a relationship. And if Charley feels something for you, then I'm sure she'll be there. Try keeping it as a friendship for now. I don't want to break confidentiality, but trust me, she's very vulnerable.'

Jinny nodded. She wasn't going to win this one. They said their goodnights and before she drove off, Jinny watched Ally let herself into her house. Once home, she parked in the drive and let herself in, locking the door securely behind her. She poured herself a glass of red wine and relaxed on the sofa, closing her eyes.

Hmm, if only Charley was here now.

She imagined kissing those soft lush pink lips. So tender. She pushed the zip of her jeans down and slid her cool slim fingers into her pants, massaging her clit. Lost in fantasy, Jinny climaxed a long deep orgasm. She opened her eyes and laughed as she realised she hadn't spilled a drop of the wine in her left hand even though her right was still in her pants.

***

Jinny

I watched Fi exit her car, take the wheelie case from the boot, and make her way over to the café. We'd agreed to meet here as Kevin being in the office made it harder to talk there. Better on my turf, where I had support – and Fi didn't deserve to be let off easy. I hoped she was going to be civil today. After all, I had caught her in the act, even after she had denied vociferously anything was going on between her and Kev. Why bloody lie? Why the betrayal? I needed closure on it all.

Fi looked over and headed straight towards me. That cold look of indifference was Fi's way of hiding anxiety. As I watched I realised there was no hurt now. Maybe that buzz for Charley had moved me past that part, showing me what little feelings I actually had left for Fi.

'I brought the files for your clients,' she said. 'Have you let them know you're going solo, or do you want me to?'

All business, hoping to avoid any real discussion.

But I wasn't going to let her off that easy. I'd lull her into a false sense of security talking about the client split, get her to relax over lunch, and then ask her what the fuck happened.

'I've already told them. They were fine with that. I did give them the choice to stay with you, but since I'd handled their accounts they were all fine to carry on with me.'

'Good. I want this to be as painless as possible for us.'

'I'm sure.' I hadn't intended that to sound sarcastic, but I could see from Fi's stoical look she'd taken it that way. 'The software is finished for Chemshare. I know they're your–'

'It's fine. I've told them you're taking them over and will provide any follow-up.'

Well that piece of generosity shocked me. That was her biggest client. Maybe she felt guilty. 'Are you sure? I wasn't expecting to keep them.'

Fi looked down, her cheeks red. 'Kevin doesn't have the expertise to deal with them and I'm too busy. They were happy to move to your company as they're pleased with everything you've done for them already. So it was the best decision for us all.'

'I'll not argue with that. Thanks.'

So not guilt, more just a bloody incompetent assistant. I wouldn't look that gift horse in the mouth, though. I waved Linda to bring us coffee. Fi pulled a file from her bag and opened it at pages requiring my signature. The lawyer had already discussed the changes with us both. Now I just needed to sign these forms and the deal was done; I'd have no more ties to Fi. Probably wouldn't ever see her again since she lived in the next town.

Linda placed the coffees down away from the papers and made a quick retreat.

'I've got the papers here.' Fi handed over a pen from her bag. Always organised. I wouldn't miss that, I loved a bit of mess and chaos. It made me realise how much of a weight had been lifted, how free I now felt. Did I ever really love her or was I just blown away by her good looks, smart brain and generosity?

'Look, Jinny, I . . .'

She was struggling with this. Well, good. I wasn't going to make it easy for her – what she did was wrong, so to hell with her.

'I'm sorry. Really, I shouldn't have done what I did. I don't even know why I did that. But I do want you to know, I hadn't actually shagged Kevin till the day you caught us.' She saw my look of disbelief and reddened some more. 'Although we had kissed, and I knew it was going to go somewhere. I thought if I just had a shag I'd get it out my system–'

I just stared at her and my silence seemed to prompt her; I'd never been silent before and she'd never talked before. We'd argue, we'd get over it. This was new. This was communication. Just way too bloody late.

'You know I'm bi. But I don't have feelings for Kevin. It was just lust. I wanted some flesh instead of silicone. I hope you can understand?'

I still said nothing; I didn't understand. I'd never felt the need to try the opposite sex because it just felt wrong. Dildos were just toys for pleasure, not stand-ins for the real thing for me.

'I don't suppose you might want to . . .?'

I think the look of horror on my face was enough to answer that question. Her eyes filled and I pulled out a serviette from the dispenser and handed it over. God, I was sympathetic today – not.

She smiled gingerly and took it with a trembling hand. 'Can you forgive me?'

I sighed long and deep. 'Maybe in time, when I forget it. If I'm honest, I think we've been drifting apart for a while, have we not?' She nodded. 'And since you were the one that shirked off my advances for a bit of nooky, I'd say you went off me before I realised you'd lost interest.' She nodded slightly again. 'I just want to know why you didn't end it then. Why did you bloody let me think I was being paranoid?'

'I don't know. I guess I didn't want to be on my own. I still loved your company. And I also worried about splitting the business up. I guess when I realised the business would be fine I started giving Kevin the come on. I didn't mean to cheat, I didn't want to lose you.' I gave her a look of 'you're joking right?' and she looked down at the soggy serviette.

'Anyway, I won't be shagging Kevin again. I still prefer women. I just needed to . . . Well, you know . . .'

I had my answer. I had closure. I was okay. No, I was better than okay. And Fi being fazed by my cool calm composure was the icing on the cake. I was glad it was over. 'Well, I think that's us done, eh?' I signed the dotted lines, took my copy and handed the documents back. She tentatively smiled and her hands shook as she put them in her bag. She smiled again and clumsily got up, screeching her chair back and drawing a few glances from the customers. Still nodding, she placed the wheelie case beside me.

'There. See you . . .'

It felt awkward, really awkward. I stood silently, giving nothing back. She nodded again, clearly understanding that this was it, before clicking her heels out the door. I let out a deep breath and smiled. I felt surprisingly free.

CHAPTER SIX

It's not your fault you're having to fix this one too. You watched her, gave her time to change, but she was weak, like the rest of them. So you have to be the responsible one. She's young, you've caught her early; she'll survive, she'll be transformed.

You feel a connection to this one. You watched her interact. You've watched her crying alone, in her room, through the gap in the curtains. She's sad and frightened of being true to how she wants to be. But you can show her a better way to be. No one else knows her like you. No one else can help her, like you can. It's your duty.

At the college campus she often sits alone, watching others, daydreaming with a sad, isolated look on her face. You've watched her from a distance as she smiles at passers-by, hoping to be accepted. You've seen her hesitate outside of doors, wanting to go in. Wanting to be part of the various lunchtime clubs that try to make everyone feel included, but her hand always hovers over the handle, she never opens the door and she never goes in. You can help her with this. You can fix her. She'll be accepted.

It's been hard to choose the right spot and time

for your intervention. She's never out at night. All her activities are in daylight hours in public places and after college she catches the bus and goes home to her parents who run a strict and orderly house. You thought you would never get your chance. You've even had to re-organise your list. Thankfully, the local nursing home, where her mother works in the kitchen, has organised an evening's entertainment show. Juniors from the local school will sing and dance to the patients, who can't sing or dance themselves and have no clue what day it is as they drool into their annual tipple. And once it's over and the geriatrics have been wheeled off to bed, she will stay behind to clear the dishes and rearrange the seating, and then you will find an opportune moment.

Now that moment has arrived. You've seen her pushing the grannies about all night. Watched as she passed around the sherry and stout, smiling kindly. Waited, while she tied up the trash to put it out on her way home. The bins are at the side of the converted sandstone building, its thick bushes and trees to the back and sides. How you love these dense, mature gardens, perfect for playing hide and seek in as a child and perfect now, for your fix.

It's easy for you to sneak up on her and get the hood on. You've tightened it just enough until she's limp in your arms. You've enough time to push a rag into her young, sweet mouth and tape it while you prepare her and yourself. It's important to take precautions. You can't have one mistake end all your good work.

Her eyes start to flicker as you put the hood back on. You part her legs. The first thrust is tight, it takes a few to break her open completely. She's awake now. You hear her sharp, ragged breath as she begins to panic, squirming underneath your weight.

She's tight and moist as you plunge deeper. Innocence and purity intensifying your thrusts. She's limp again as you empty yourself into your condom. It annoys you that you need to use one, but you can't leave DNA. You'd like to lie here for a bit, enjoying the tight warmth but you have to finish the ritual. You're still in her, pinning her to the wet, leafy earth, as you reach for the blade that is tucked inside the rucksack. Sliding out of her you can hear her whimper; she thinks it's over. The blade glints as you plunge it into the soft young flesh above her dark triangle and you hear her muffled scream.

Your fix is done. Another name to strike from the list.

CHAPTER SEVEN

Ally

It was 11.35 p.m. and even though I could've happily stayed up all night binge-watching another three episodes of my current favourite conspiracy thriller on Netflix, I decided, reluctantly, to switch off and go to bed. Midway through brushing my teeth my mobile started vibrating on my bedside table.

'Hawo,' I answered through a mouthful of slobbery toothpaste.

'Ally?' A husky, male voice that I recognised it instantly. It was the DCI. God, his voice was as sexy as his looks.

'Yes. S– sorry, I was just brushing my teeth, I didn't want to miss the call.'

'That's okay. It's Nick Daniels. Ally, I'm sorry it's late but we need you again at the hospital.'

'There's been another rape.' I knew it was more of a statement than question.

'Yes. I don't want to say any more over the phone. Can you come?'

'Of course, I'll leave now.' I replied immediately.

'Good. Come to intensive care. I'll meet you there. And Ally . . . be careful.'

I almost swooned over how genuinely concerned he seemed, but pushing romantic thoughts aside, I cleaned up my face and hastily got ready. So much for going to bed early tonight.

Nick was in the corridor of the intensive care unit when I arrived. He was deep in conversation with DI Jake De Stefano, when I slipped through the automatic doors which were currently switched to manual, preventing them from opening and closing every time someone came too near to the sensor. A policewoman stood inside, scrutinising all visitors. She checked my badge and pointed down the corridor to where Nick stood. Before I caught up to them, Jake nodded to Nick and walked off into the nurses' station. I was glad I didn't need to interact with him. I didn't know him, but there was something I didn't like.

'Ally, sorry for bringing you out on a Sunday night.' Nick's hand reached out to shake mine and then slid it along my arm, guiding me into a treatment area where the nurses prepared the intravenous antibiotics and other drugs. The room had a large window looking into the ward, where patients were screened from each other, surrounded by beeping machines that recorded every pulse and breath, and endless tubes leading from bags into veins.

'Bed three. Robyn Carruthers. Eighteen. College student. Raped, stabbed and left to die in bushes at the Woodend Care Home. They'd had a school group in to entertain the residents and she'd been helping out.' Nick dragged his hand through his hair that had flopped into his eyes.

'Oh no, not again. I'm guessing if she's in the ICU her condition is pretty serious?' I swallowed, trying to take in the scene, wondering why this nastiness was happening in our normally quiet, picturesque town. Standing as close to Nick as I could without invading his personal space, I had a strong urge to breathe him in, to take in his male scent to fill my lungs with his essence. God, it had been ages since I'd felt this sort of attraction to a guy. What was wrong with me? I probably just needed a good shag. I was allowing my sexual frustrations to cloud the seriousness of the situation and that was not me.

'She has similar injuries to Dr Garby.' Nick's conversation jolted me back to my senses. 'She lost a lot of blood and, like Gill, had to have a hysterectomy. We think she had a gag in her mouth and she choked, because it looks like she may have aspirated some vomit. She's more stable, thankfully. They're about to take the breathing tube out now and she's been sedated, but that'll be wearing off soon.'

I nodded, watching as nurses wheeled a trolley next to the victim's bed and drew the curtains. 'Is her family here? Have they been told?'

'Yes, they're in the relative's room with the liaison police officer and the charge nurse. They're pretty shaken up and they've asked the minister to come in and say some prayers with them.'

'I see. They're lucky to have a faith where they can direct their hurt and grief. I'm sure John will be a good support to them.'

'John? Ah, the minister? Not your thing – religion?'

'Each to their own, Nick. Look, Robyn's stirring.' I nodded in the direction of the nurses as they pulled back the screens and finished tidying the bedsheets and locker. The door opened and a nurse stuck her head in.

'That's Miss Carruthers coming round now, Inspector. I'm just going to let her parents come in to see her briefly and if she's stable over the next few hours, we will move her to a private room in the high dependency area.'

'Nurse er . . . Jones.' Nick glanced quickly at her name badge. 'Wait, before you do that, myself and Counsellor Canessa will speak to her first. It's important for the investigation.'

'Of course, Inspector. Let me know when you are finished.' Nurse Jones retreated, leaving us to enter the ward area.

Robyn Carruthers looked small, petite and much younger than her eighteen years. Her light, fair hair was a tangled mess and her face was pale, almost invisible, against the pillow. Stiff, white hospital sheets were tucked under pale arms that were decorated with fresh, angry, red scratches and bruises. Her neck had dark red bruising all round it.

Same as Gill.

I reached out, taking her thin white hand in mine and leaning over. I quietly said her name, careful to avoid anything that may frighten her.

Robyn swallowed a few times, wincing slightly as she did so, and flickered open her eyes. She squinted against the brightness, even though the artificial lighting in the department was kept deliberately low for the comfort of the patients. After what seemed like minutes, but was really only a few seconds, Robyn's strikingly blue eyes refocused on me and then Nick. She looked scared, confused. Her eyes darted about, trying to take in the surroundings. She whimpered and tried to move but clearly became aware of the pain in her lower abdomen, wincing again.

'Robyn, you're in hospital. You're safe now. You were attacked and needed surgery. I'm Nick Daniels, the detective looking after you, and this is Allison Canessa, she's a counsellor. We want to find out who did this to you. Do you feel up to telling us what you remember?' Nick looked anxiously at Robyn, hoping she could give him something, anything that could help.

I squeezed her hand tighter, letting her know she wasn't alone – or just hoping she could give us the name of who did this to her.

A solitary tear ran down the side of her face. 'I c– can't do this. Please . . . leave me alone.' She sobbed and pulled her hand away from mine, shaking her head, trying to deny the reality of her assault.

'Robyn, we need your help. If you could–' I put my hand onto Nick's shoulder and shook my head, indicating to leave the questioning, for now at least. He sighed in resignation.

'Your parents are here, Robyn. They want to see you. Is that okay?' I asked gently; maybe they could find out more. She started sobbing again, but managed to nod to the question.

Nick and I left the room and stood in a quiet corner of the corridor. I understood his need to question, time was critical for the investigation, but I also understood the victim; they would talk in their own time and backing them into a corner could hamper their recovery.

'I'll get the parents, maybe they can find out more,' I said, trying to ease his impatience.

'They won't know what to ask, Ally. Time is of the essence here. The sooner we get details, the sooner we can start to put the pieces together, find witnesses, put a time-frame together. And stop him from . . . Damn!'

'I know you're frustrated, but she needs time to focus, to put the pieces together herself. She's just out of surgery and we'll get–' My sentence was broken by the sound of the doors being flung open and a loud, bellowing male voice.

'Where is she? Where's my daughter? We've waited in that room long enough and we need to see her. Now.' Mr Carruthers was stomping down the corridor ahead of Mrs Carruthers, who was being visibly supported by Reverend John Proctor. Nick quickly stepped in, taking control of the situation.

'Mr and Mrs Carruthers, I'm the lead detective, Nick Daniels. I spoke to you on the phone. We were just about to come and get you. I know the charge nurse has been keeping you up to speed with Robyn.'

'Shouldn't you be out looking for this monster?' Mrs Carruthers spat the words at Nick. She looked extremely distressed as she leant further into the minister, who stroked her arm in sympathy.

'They just need to see their daughter, to see she is okay, to pray for her.' John looked beseechingly towards Nick, then me. 'Ally, it's good to see a familiar face in this troubling time.' He patted my shoulder and turned back to Nick.

'Of course,' Nick said. 'You must be desperate to see her. We're just trying to establish some details. Maybe Mrs Carruthers, Mr Carruthers, you could ask her what she saw, any details that can help?'

'Surely you must know something? Didn't anyone see anything or anyone?' John asked impatiently.

'We're still looking at the evidence so far. Were you at the residential home tonight Reverend? Did you see anything suspicious?'

'No, I wasn't. I helped the kids set up in the afternoon, but I have a funeral on Tuesday that I have to prepare for, so I left early. Sorry, I know that's not much help. I wish I'd seen something to help put this beast behind bars, but I didn't. Let's go in Kathy, Mike.' John nodded to us both as he escorted Robyn's parents into the ward.

I wasn't sure if Nick had no evidence or didn't want to give anything away, but I too wanted to find out more.

We watched as they went into the ward. Mrs Carruthers took one look at her daughter and turned to sob into John's chest, while Mr Carruthers put his hands over his mouth. Robyn was still groggy from the anaesthetic and morphine and was slipping back into a sedated sleep. She wasn't going to be saying much for a while. As we watched, I used the time to question Nick.

'Who found her?' I started.

'An emergency call on her mobile was made at about eight fifteen.'

'She made the call?'

'We don't know, Ally. Look, I know what you're digging at, and yes, it's the same MO as Gill Garby, as far as we can see, anyway. There are some things we need to check, but so far, it looks like the same guy.'

'So we have a serial rapist out there, Nick? And not your typical, garden variety, run-of-the-mill rapist either. This one gets a kick out of mutilating his victims.' I was scared. I knew forensics from Robyn would take some time to come back but I needed to know if we had clues on who this could be. 'What forensics did we get from Gill? Any DNA or anything?'

'No DNA, no evidence. He's obviously used a condom. He's smart, tidy.' Nick looked thoughtful as he spoke, maybe hoping that he'd think of something he hadn't already covered.

'And no one saw anything tonight?'

'I've got Jake and the team out asking folk that were at Woodend working. And we're checking names and addresses of parents or visitors who were in the area dropping or collecting kids or seeing the show. It'll take time.'

'So, what are you going to say to the press? People are gonna be frightened there's a serial rapist in the–'

'Whoa, Ally! We're not saying anything about a serial anything to the press. And the family don't want it known their daughter was raped. They're very religious–'

'What? Nick, people need to know. Even without naming the victim. They need to be aware, to be more careful. And anyway, it's so bloody obvious it's the same person, the press will put it together. And if you withhold the facts and someone else gets hurt, they'll be pointing fingers at you.' I could feel the barriers going up between us. I felt exasperated, how could he not see this?

'Ally, I understand your concerns, but stop already. The press will be told there's been another rape and that people should be more vigilant. Sometimes though, it's more important for the investigation to withhold key information, otherwise we get the public behaving like vigilantes or calling us every minute with every piece of useless information that wastes our time.'

Nick looked tired and I felt guilty for rattling his cage, but I knew I was right and I wasn't backing down over this. I shook my head, turned on my heel and walked away. Maybe I could try again with Robyn.

By the time I got back to the bed the nurses were preparing to move her to the high dependency unit, one floor down. They disconnected monitors and in one synchronised movement, her bed and intravenous pumps were wheeled into the lift, while I, plus John and her parents, took the stairs. Nick, following, made sure another officer was stationed outside and he left the liaison policewoman to keep communication flowing between police, family and hospital staff. I took my turn sitting with Robyn while her family got coffee and John headed back to church. She looked so fragile as she flitted in and out of sleep or taking small sips of water to moisten her mouth.

When her mother left to go to the toilet and her father was quietly snoring in the armchair, I stole my chance to question her again. Gently, broaching the subject but letting her know that she could prevent another rape, I asked her what happened.

'I didn't see anything. He grabbed me from behind and put something over my head. It was so tight, on my neck . . . and then . . .' She touched the purplish, red bruises to her neck, remembering the events. Tears silently flowed and her cheeks began to redden. She glanced over to her father, checking to see if he was listening, obviously relieved he was still asleep. 'I must have passed out. When I woke, I had something in my mouth that was making me choke.' She glanced at her father again and whispered, 'And he was . . . he was in me. And then the pain. He . . . he stabbed me.' The words sputtered out of her mouth and she turned her head away from me abruptly; she was angry that I had finally made her say it.

'Robyn, please. I know this is hard. Please, one more question. Please, Robyn?' I implored. 'Who made the call to the police? Was it you? Did you use your mobile to call for help?'

'Call? What call?' Robyn turned her head away just as her mother returned.

'What's going on? What did she say? Robyn, honey are you okay?' Robyn's mother looked at me accusingly as I got up.

'I need to make a call and get to work. It's been a long night. I'll check in later. Thank you, Robyn.'

On my way into work I passed the closed road

signs and I could make out the blue forensics tent and the white overalls of the team as they examined the crime area around Woodend. It would be there for several days, as it had been for Gill's case. I stopped off at Jin's café for a take away coffee.

'Hi Roz, a soya cappuccino to go, please. Eh, where's Jin?' I asked looking around.

'Oh she's working from the flat this morning before going round to the demo.'

'Demo? What demo?'

'At the hotel. Seems like the Bishoptons weren't too happy about their clientele's sexuality . . . or something like that. I'd have thought Jinny would've said.'

'She might have mentioned it, but I've been pretty full on lately. No worries. I'll text her.' I grabbed my coffee and headed to work.

I was early so I unlocked the centre and had a quick look at my schedule. First client wouldn't be in till ten. I was relieved that'd give me time to speak to Nick. I dialled his number.

'Daniels.' Nick sounded tired.

'Nick, it's Ally. I managed to confirm a couple of things with Robyn this morning. She definitely had something over her head, like Gill. She also had something in her mouth to gag her. And Nick . . . she never made that call either.' We both knew what that meant; the rapist wanted their victims found.

'Good work, Ally. Look, I've gotta go, the team are waiting for an update and I've gotta say something to the press.' He sounded harassed.

'Oh, er . . . right. I understand. I just wanted to let you know.'

'I appreciate that. Thanks, Ally.'

I heard someone come in to the centre and peeked out. It was Sharon. I texted Jinny first before going out to greet her.

There's been another rape. I can't talk now, don't say anything to anyone. Busy now. Talk later. Be careful. Xx

OMFG! Another. I'm heading to demo shortly. Speak soon. You be careful too. Xxx

***

Jinny

As I pushed my way to the back of the crowd, I was totally fucking delighted to see the huge turnout for the protest outside the Gables Hotel. There was no sign of either of the Bishoptons. Hiding away from the crowd, I expected. I was bloody disgusted that in this current climate of inclusivity, we still had idiots like Bill Bishopton acting as if it was the fifties when being gay was a crime. Bill had taken it upon himself to unceremoniously toss a gay couple out of *their own* wedding reception when he saw that the groom, Den, wasn't a groom. He wouldn't refund them either. Their guests called the police, but the officers couldn't do anything to change Bishopton's mind, and just suggested to the newly married couple they take them to court. So that's what they were doing – as well as shaming them publicly. At least a hundred people were spilling off the large driveway and into the gardens. I joined in the chanting, 'Equal treatment, gay rights, any gender can stay the night!'

From my vantage point at the higher end of the drive I could see news vans and reporters filming the crowd who were waving a sheet up and down with the rhyming slogan painted in red capitals. I recognised some of the faces, customers that frequented the café: the Les Bikers, they called themselves; a group of lesbians that socialised together on Harley adventure weekends. Most people though, I had never seen before. I had no problem with letting people know I was gay, but I didn't go around telling everyone I met. The regulars at the café knew me from when I lived here before with Beth, but there were a great many new faces I didn't recognise since coming back to town. And I did get a warm, fuzzy feeling from all the heartfelt support for this occasion.

The reporter interviewing the couple waved someone to come closer. I saw it was John Proctor, the minister, and then I got a thrill as I noticed Charley tagging along. I didn't want to get too close to the cameras so I hung back, standing to the side. If Charley looked back, she'd see me.

'God knows I'm right!' was bellowed from behind me as the crowd all turned to watch Bill Bishopton shout from a second storey window. 'Remember Sodom and Gomorrah. They were punished with eternal fire.'

The crowd retaliated with their slogan. Some shouted other quotes from the bible, about God loving all his children, and the like. I was never religious.

'Minister, you should know this!' Bill shouted over the noise, his voice echoing down the driveway. 'Levictus 18:22, says, "Thou shalt not lie with mankind, as with womankind: it is an abomination."'

I saw the minister shake his head and talk into the microphone the reporter was holding. I'd no idea what he was saying but it looked like he was arguing the point. Charley noticed me at that point and gave me a wave. I waved back, watching as she turned to respond to the reporter. Good for her. I liked this woman even more.

'Levictus 20:13, "If a man lies with another man and a woman lies with a woman they have committed a detestable act; Levictus says they'll be put to death."'

I just hated those bible-touting twats. I was sure I could find plenty of bible quotes for anything I wanted to justify doing.

What a prick.

I hadn't realised I'd said the latter out loud until the man beside me in a pride T-shirt and rainbow-dyed buzz-cut said that was an insult to genitalia.

'Corninthians 6:9-10 said, "effeminates and homosexuals will not inherit the kingdom of God."'

More bible quotes from the opposing argument were hurled back from the crowd.

'God created Adam and Eve. Not Eve and Eve or Adam and Adam!' Bob Bishopton roared. 'Get off my property. You're all sinners. God will punish you for your degrading behaviour. Mark my words. You can't hide from God.'

The crowd tried to drown him out, but he closed the window and the curtains, and the original chant started up again.

'Threw his own daughter out,' rainbow buzz-cut told me. 'I was at school with her – Micky. We had planned to go to the same college, but when her dad found out she was gay, he tried to strangle her.'

I was shocked; I hadn't heard that. 'Are you sure?'

'Yeah. We'd kept in touch. I saw the bruises he left. Seems her mother tried to stop him and she got a black eye for it. But Micky got just tossed out with nothing. Wasn't even allowed to take her stuff.' He

89

shook his head in disgust, joining in the chanting again.

I *had* heard that Bishopton's daughter went off to London to stay with her girlfriend's parents, and was still married to that same girl. The gossip mill in the café kept you updated on things like that. Both women were lawyers now, with their own practice, and according to rumour, never came home, not even to visit her mother. To be honest, since Anne got used as Bill's punch bag, I doubt she'd have been any help, anyway. Probably afraid of being tossed out herself.

I was busy in my musings when I felt a light tap on my shoulder. I knew who it was before I turned around. The waft of light vanilla that signalled Charley's presence caused my heart to beat faster.

'Hey you.' I heard the nervous tremor in my voice. And Ally's voice in my head warning me not to seem too eager, but damn, I felt like a schoolgirl talking to her first crush. 'Great to see you here. I see John's being interviewed still.'

'Yeah.' She laughed. 'He's countering the argument with a few appropriate bible quotes of his own.'

'It's just bloody shocking what the Bishoptons did, though.'

'Yeah, the family had paid all up front for the reception. Didn't get any of their money back, and all the guests that were going to stay the night had to leave in support of the couple, and they didn't get a refund either.'

'What makes anyone think that is normal – or even Christian,' I added, wondering if Charley was – unlike me – religious. 'That type of behaviour is beyond me.'

'Bill Bishopton deserves to be taken to court. He deserves all the bad publicity. I've heard they haven't had many bookings since this all was exposed.'

'Yeah, I heard that too.' The chanting got louder again, making it harder to talk. I leaned in close to her ear, her delicate ear. I wanted to place a kiss just behind it. Ally would be furious with me. 'Time for a coffee?'

Charley looked at her brother, who was surrounded by reporters and cameras. She nodded. 'I'll text him to let him know I'll see him later at The Manse. He's got a pastoral counselling session there. But plenty time for a coffee.'

I led the way through the crowd, feeling Charley gripping onto my jacket so as not to lose me. I loved that, it felt right; a comfortable connection. Once through the throng and out the gates she walked alongside me, closely, as we got to my car.

'We can go to the café first, then I can drop you off at The Old Manse later, if you want?'

'If you don't mind. I came with John, so that'd be great.' Charley jumped into the passenger side of my Kia Sportage as I unlocked the doors. 'Great colour,' she said, admiring my car. 'I love electric blue. I think it's my favourite colour.'

'Mine too! Then I love a nice deep, rich red.'

Charley laughed. 'Oh my God, so do I. I love to see red and blue together, too. The contrast does things to my eyes.'

'Yeah, I know what you mean.'

In the café, I placed Charley into one of the private seating booths and ordered our coffees from Linda. I picked up the lunch menu, even though it was still a bit early for lunch, but maybe she'd stay longer if she decided to eat. I just wanted to get to know her more. I wasn't going to flirt, but I do want to be her friend. I liked Charley.

'I brought the lunch menu, if you fancied a bite.' I planted myself down opposite her.

'Actually, I didn't bring any money. Do you know if they take Apple pay here?'

'They have apple pie.'

'Good one,' Charley laughed.

'They do, but please, this is on the house. The place is mine.'

'The café is yours? I thought you were a software developer.' She blushed. 'I'd asked Ally. Sorry, I hope you don't mind.'

'Of course not. I'm chuffed you asked.' She blushed even more. I'm glad it wasn't just me that felt timorous. 'The café was left to me by my first love. She died of breast cancer.'

Charley looked shocked. 'Oh, I'm sorry to hear that, Jinny.' Her hand patted mine, then pulled back nervously.

'It was a long time ago. But I do love it here. I've got a great manager, so it runs itself. I live in the cottage attached around the back. And I *am* a software developer for my other job.'

'It's great in here.' Charley looked around at the American-diner interior.

'I've always like that chic diner style,' I admitted, hoping for her approval.

'It's very cheery and I love the private booths.'

'Me too. I've only kept it fresh. It's not changed much since Beth ran it, other than change the name to The Cauldron to keep in with Covenston's rich witch history.' I dangled the menu in front of her.

She looked at it, then at me, and a smile lit her face. 'Well, if you don't mind, I'd love a home-baked scone with jam and cream. The photo on the menu is screaming at me.'

I laughed. 'Good choice. One of my favourites

too. They are freshly baked, and from what I can smell, a batch has just landed.'

'The whole menu is vegan?' Charley asked, examining it on both sides.

'Yep. Beth made all her own recipes and I've added a few of my own. You'll like the cream. It's oat-based and most people say if they didn't know, they'd think it was dairy.'

'Ooh, I can't wait.'

I went over to the counter and helped myself to the scones and jam dishes, and asked Linda to get me the cream from the fridge. She wiggled her eyebrows at me as she placed it on my tray. 'Getting over Fiona okay?'

'It's not like that,' I admonished, although I could feel my cheeks warming. Linda just lifted her eyebrows higher and nodded slowly. 'It's not . . . She's a friend.'

'Yeah. Good.' Linda turned back into the kitchen before I could retaliate.

'That smells like heaven.' Charley grabbed the nearest scone, cutting it open. She lathered it in jam and cream and took a bite. A bit of cream stuck to the edge of her mouth. I wanted to lick it off. Instead, I just pointed to my mouth.

'Cream . . .' I said, as her tongue flicked out and licked it off.

'Divine. You're right. I wouldn't know this wasn't dairy. I won't ask for the recipe. It'll give me an excuse to come back. I've never been in here before.'

'We're the only totally vegan café in town. But we're busy as hell most days, so I guess it's not just vegans that come here to eat.'

'Well, if all your food is as good and fresh as this, it isn't any wonder.' She stuffed another bite in

93

and rolled her eyes in enjoyment. 'Mmm, delish.'

I ate mine and we talked for over an hour. We got on well, but I didn't want to push it. Ally was right. It would be nice just to be friends first and see if it led to anything else. I was sure Charley felt the same about me, so I was taken by surprise when she just blurted out, 'I was raped.' I didn't say anything. She carried on before I even got a chance to think about how to respond.

'That's why I was seeing Ally. I was young – it was fifteen years ago. I just wanted you to know. You see, I am gay, but after that, I've never had a relationship.'

'I . . .' I was lost for words. '. . . I'm sorry that happened to you, Charley. You don't need to tell me any–'

'Actually, I want to, if you don't mind hearing it.'

I patted *her* hand this time. I didn't let it linger, that felt too early. 'I'm happy to listen. Anytime, Charley. I don't know how to say this, but, well, I feel like we click. I feel like I've known you for years.'

She smiled, and it reached her eyes. 'I feel the same. I think that's why I'm ready to talk about it to you. I've only ever told Ally, and John knows, but I've never told anyone else. You're the first that I want to tell all the gory details to. And I feel it says I'm moving on.' She nodded, as if accepting the realisation herself. 'And it was so easy to tell you that.' She grabbed my hand and squeezed it. 'I'd better get back.' She stood up and put her coat on. 'See you at the coven?'

I nodded as I stood up too. I was her ride; I think she'd forgotten. When she saw me stand, she laughed.

'I forgot. You said you'd drive me.' Charley

slipped her arm into mine as we went out the door. I felt a warmth rush through my whole body and a lump of pure emotion at the back of my throat. Deep down, I knew that Charley was moving on. And I so hoped I was going to be part of her future – as a friend, or more.

CHAPTER EIGHT

Ally

I was relieved it was Friday, soon to be the weekend. I really needed a couple of days off to recharge my batteries. If my energy deflated anymore I'd need to strap a bed to my back. I left the centre around ten, after checking that Steph, one of our part-time counsellors, was up to speed on today's client list. I was grateful that she could manage an extra day this week, giving me time to see Robyn at the hospital. I also wanted to find out if Nick was any further forward in the investigation and, if I was to be honest, I really wanted to see him again. I'd spoken to Gill a few times since her assault. Although still recovering from the surgery she had, she was surprisingly well, both physically and emotionally, considering what she'd been through. We agreed that she would see me for a few sessions, but she felt that her acceptance of the trauma coupled with her professional understanding, meant that long-term counselling wouldn't be warranted. In this circumstance I did agree, but I knew that I'd keep in close contact just in case there were any hiccups. I also knew she wasn't one for sympathy, so I didn't want her trading good mental health for fear of being pitied.

Nick had also spoken with Gill, but he hadn't uncovered any more information. She was a well-respected GP within the community and had no personal or professional threats that she could think off. Gill had agreed to assist in a reconstruction of the events, using actors as the victim and assailant. The plan, however, had been put on the back burner when Robyn got raped and the focus of investigation switched to her.

I thought more about the investigation while I drove to the hospital. Wiggling my toes in my loose boots, enjoying the warm air blowing out of the heater in my Mini Cooper, I decided to remind Nick to do the reconstruction of Gill's rape. Maybe a reconstruction of Robyn's events, too, if she agreed. Someone must have seen something.

At the entrance to Robyn's room I showed my ID to a different policewoman. She had been moved again, this time to another private room on one of the surgical wards. She had been hoping to get home but an infection in her hysterectomy wound kept her here.

Hysterectomy at eighteen, good God, what a poor soul. Why? How could this happen? What sort of man could hate a woman this much?

I sighed inwardly, hoping my face wasn't leaking the horror of my thoughts as I entered her room.

'Robyn, you're looking better.' I wasn't being completely honest, but telling her she still looked like crap at death's door wasn't going to help her heal.

'Thanks Ally.' She smiled weakly. 'I'm glad you came, actually.'

'Oh yeah?'

'I wanted to say sorry for not being very open on the day of . . . I knew you were just trying to get information to help the investigation, to help me . . .'

'Robyn, you have nothing to be sorry for. You almost lost your life. You were hurt. I get it. I'm a counsellor, Robyn. I've seen people in all kinds of troubling scenarios. I understand.'

'I . . . I was a virgin,' she blurted into her hands. 'H . . . he stole that from me. And now, I can't even have children if I ever wanted to. I c-can't get over this. How can I, after what he's done?' Sobs racked her body. I understood why. She was a young woman, just starting out and he stole her innocence, her dreams.

'Robyn, it may not seem like it now because of what you have just been through. It's still raw. You have a grieving process to go through. And you *will* get through it, I promise you. No matter how tough it may seem at times, you will get through it. I'll be there for you.' I took her hand to seal my promise. At that same time I also made a promise to myself that whoever did this to Gill and Robyn would be caught, no matter what.

Robyn and I spoke until she looked too tired to carry on, going over what she remembered of her rape and working to begin her trauma counselling.

'I think we'd better call it a day, Robyn. You look beat and you've done some good work. It's a start.'

'Do you think it's the same guy, Ally?' She looked concerned.

'Same guy?' I knew fine well what she was getting at, but was stalling while I worked out the best way to answer.

'Yeah. The same one who raped that doctor, too? It is, isn't it? Why haven't the reporters on the telly said it was the same guy?'

'It might be, Robyn. I don't know. The police are still doing their investigation and they won't want the public or the media jumping to any conclusions. I'm actually on my way to see DI Daniels now.'

'I'm scared. People'll find out I've been raped. They'll talk. My parents said I'll be embarrassed.'

'You didn't ask for this. You have nothing to be embarrassed about. I can talk to your parents, Robyn.'

'No. Don't say anything, Ally. Reverend Proctor said he'll talk to them.'

'I'm glad he's on your side. I'm sure he can support you and your parents, and I'll be here too, of course.' I knew it was too soon, too raw, to ask if we could do a reconstruction. Perhaps if she spoke with Gill, it might help, but not now, I decided.

I made my way to the police station to see Nick, sending a text to say I was coming in and he was fine with that. I was waved in through the front desk and made my way to his office on the second floor. The door was open and I was disappointed to see he shared an office with Jake De Stefano. They were chatting as I rapped my knuckles off the doorframe to let them know I was there.

'Ally, hi. I almost forgot you were coming in. We've been busy, eh, Jake?' Nick dragged a chair closer to his desk. 'Sit, please. Do you want coffee?'

He forgot I was coming in? So much for thinking we could be an item.

'Oh, no thanks. It's just a quick visit.' I smiled at both of them as they each took their own seats behind their desks. It wasn't a large room, both desks were joined together, facing each other in front of a very large window, which overlooked the town's post office car park. The room was lined with filing cabinets and bookcases, with a large white board behind Nick's desk. It showed current investigations with specific, important details underlined or highlighted in red ink. Right now, Robyn and Gill's cases were all over the board, photos of specific relevance numbered and marked to point out contrasting evidence in both cases.

'I was wondering if you had any more leads, or are any closer to catching this guy?'

'There's no new forensics, if that's what you mean? We've jack-shit, to be honest.' Nick looked worried, pushing his hair back the way he usually did. I hoped I wasn't drooling as I watched his movements.

'What about the door-to-doors? Or the people in and around Woodend – anything?'

'One of the nursing assistants thought they heard something in the bushes when they finished their shift. They said it sounded like a squeal, but they just put it down to the neighbour's cat and didn't bother looking.' Jake looked frustrated at the lack of anything solid.

'I think we should be doing Gill's reconstruction as soon as possible,' I said looking between both of them.

'Yeah,' Jake agreed, his dark eyes meeting mine. 'I was saying the exact same thing to Nick just before you got here.'

Maybe he wasn't so hostile. After all, I thought, he had no reason to be. 'I think we really need to get more information out there, warn the public. Young women need to take more precautions when they're out. They need to know there's a serial rapist out there, Nick.' I looked at him, my eyes pleading, hoping that Jake might back me up.

'Ally, there's a fine balance here,' Jake offered.

'Nick is right to be cautious over this. He's already given the journos plenty for now.'

'We've told them two women have been assaulted and raped. We've implied there might be a connection,' Nick interjected. 'We've told women to be careful. But we're not telling them the finer details about the victims' heads being covered or how they were stabbed in the same way. Right now, we're trying to figure out any reason why *these* particular women; it could be random.' Nick looked exasperated, but not as much as I did.

'But if people knew more, if they were thinking about a serial rapist, they might start to be more suspicious. It might turn up more leads if they see their husbands, boyfriends or sons doing things out of character. And what about the stabbings? I was thinking about that. It's like he has some personal vendetta . . . Maybe he doesn't want them having children–'

'For Christ's sake, Ally, of course he has a vendetta against women. He's out there raping them. And as I already said, if we give the media more we'll be swamped with calls from bitter wives and jealous girlfriends, not to mention a town full of nosey reporters. It might drive the perp into hiding and we'll lose the trail.' Nick hit back furiously.

'What trail, Nick? There are no leads, you've jack-shit, remember!' I grabbed my coat from the back of the chair, knocking it over as I left. I was raging. How many more women were going to get hurt?

'Ally. Ally wait up.' Nick shouted after me as I started along the corridor.

'What, Nick? Look, I get it. You want me to butt out. But I'm concerned. I'm the one that's got to see these women for the next x number of years, the victims whose lives are destroyed.' My eyes started to well up.

Nick sighed, but it wasn't out of anger, it was empathy. He took my arm and guided me into an empty conference room, away from the prying stares from the rest of his team who witnessed my showdown from their offices. I didn't care.

'Ally, I agree with you that there's more to this than just some fucking creep raping women for his perverted fun. That's why we gotta take it slow. There might be something that we just aren't seeing yet. You've a good eye. Why don't you sit in with us this afternoon for the team debrief? I've called someone in from CID to look at what we have. What do you think?'

His warm hand came up to my face and cupped my cheek while his thumb wiped away a solitary tear that streaked my face. It felt personal. Close. But I was still angry so I moved away and nodded to let him know I'd be there. I left the room and carried on along the corridor, wanting to look back to see if he was watching me, but I didn't.

I decided I needed to blow off steam and I knew that Jinny usually ran in the afternoon before dinner. I decided to text her.

Are you running later? Can I join you? It's my turn for a rant □

Well wasn't wanting to run alone cos of rapes, but if you want to run that'd be great. See you at 4.30 at café □♀🔑

***

102

Jinny

I must admit I was really bloody apprehensive about going to the refuge to deliver a workshop on internet safety, but Charley had asked me and I really wanted to see her again, so I said yes. And I was glad I did when I saw her big welcoming smile.

'Jinny, I'm so glad you agreed to do this,' she said. 'A few of the women here have run away from abusive relationships and are afraid of being stalked online. Most don't use the internet at all because they're afraid their exes will find out where they are. Even to the point they won't let their children online to do their homework.'

'Bloody hell, that's just shite.' I noticed Charley flinch and realised I was swearing-again. 'Sorry for the swearing. It's been a terrible habit. That's why I designed the swear app, so I'd learn to curb it.'

'Oh, I'm just not used to it – having been brought up in a strict religious environment. And I never swear here or in front of John.'

'I'm sorry. Really. I'll watch my tongue. I'm worse when I'm nervous or angry.'

'What've you got to be nervous about here? The talk?'

I smiled and bent my head so she wouldn't see my cheeks heating up. 'I . . . I just . . . Well, I was nervous about seeing you.'

'Me? No way. I'm the nervous one.' She came closer, on her toes, and whispered in my ear. 'I actually racked my brains to think up a reason to see you again, so when someone asked me if I would go online for them I found my reason to call you. So I'm the nervous one!'

I took a deep breath and tried to relax. I felt better knowing that.

'Come on. I'll introduce you and leave you to it.'

'Okay. Thanks. I'll be fine doing the talk. You don't need to leave, in fact, it might help if you listen just in case they ask questions later.'

'Okay. If you're okay with that I'll sit in.'

'Hel–' I rolled my eyes. 'I'd love that.'

Charley shook her head and jokingly slapped my arm at my near slip of the tongue. I followed her through to the room where a projector was set up for me to plug my laptop in to.

'The password for Wi-Fi is 'refuge',' Charley informed me as she handed me the projector cable.

I relaxed immediately after I started my talk. This was my speciality. I knew it inside out, and I had taught computer classes when I was doing my degree at uni, so I felt comfortable in a teaching role. All the eager faces stared at me, Charley's included. I spent forty minutes talking, allowing questions as I went along and then stayed behind to answer individual questions. These were more personal: women worried they could be traced even if they weren't on social media; a teenager worried that staying in touch with her mother on social media under a different name would lead her abusive stepfather to her door; a mum wanting to know how to use parental controls for her ten year old son. I dealt with each of them and gave them my business card in case they needed to get in touch. Charley stood at the back, with John, waiting for me to finish. I packed up my laptop as Charley came forward to thank me.

'That was excellent. If you don't mind, I think we should run that regularly. John – can we pay for talks like this out of the refuge fund?'

'Please.' I held my hand up before John could talk. 'I'd be happy to do this on a regular basis as a volunteer.'

John smiled warmly and accepted quickly. 'I'll never look a gift horse in the mouth. Thank you, Jinny. I'd be grateful. I only heard some of your talk, but what I heard was illuminating. I'm a bit old-fashioned when it comes to modern tech. I leave all that to Anne – Anne Bishopton. My assistant. I'd be lost without her. We get a quick turnover here. Would it be realistic to ask you in every four to six weeks or so?'

'Sure, I can do that.'

'Are you local? I've not seen you at church or anything. I know you're Ally's sister, but I thought she said you lived over in Wintersham?'

'I was there, John, until just a few weeks ago.'

'Jinny fell out with her girlfriend, so she moved back here to be beside Ally.'

'I'm sorry to hear about your break up. If you need to talk to anyone–' John laughed and shook his head. 'I know your sister is a counsellor, but if you feel you want to talk to someone else, someone who doesn't know you, and can be objective, my door is always open.'

'Thanks, John. That's really decent of you, but I'm fine. Ally has helped, and to be honest, I think we were over for a while. It just took a crisis to realise that. But honestly, I'm good.'

'Well, thank you once again for doing this. No doubt I'll see you next time you're over. If you'll excuse me, please, I see Anne is trying to get my attention.'

Anne Bishopton was standing in the doorway being nosey rather than trying to get John's attention. I think he realised that and was being polite.

Charley led me out to my car. 'I guess I'll see you later then. I really loved you being here.'

'I must admit, I really felt I helped. I am so

pleased you asked me. I'll add in the questions folk asked tonight to the next talk.'

'Great. Listen, I hope you're okay about what I said earlier?' I must've looked confused. 'About the swearing.'

'Shi– Oh, fu– Argh, it's going to be hard, but please give me a slap if I do it again.'

Charley laughed. 'I'll do that.'

I watched her go back into the refuge in my rear-view mirror as I drove off. I felt happy. So fuckity-fuck.

***

Ally

The debrief room was cramped and overly stuffy. I silently cursed myself for putting on my warmer sweater and hoped no one would notice that my cheeks and nose were turning the same shade of red as the offending jumper. Was every officer from the station in the room? I scanned the room discreetly, taking in the sea of faces. All heads were turned to listen to the Detective Chief Superintendent - an older, tall man with grey hair and glasses perched at the end of his nose. He appeared to easily command respect from his junior officers, standing only long enough to stress the importance of finding the maniac responsible for 'shitting in his backyard' and bringing him to justice as quickly as possible to protect any more women from becoming his prey. He then introduced the two CID officers sitting close to the top end of the long table. They were here to support, advice and to possibly take over if the situation warranted it. I wondered how *bad*, bad was, for them to take over. Surely this was it?

Nick then stood up and, after introducing himself, brought up a picture on the large video screen: Gill, the rapist's first victim. He explained who she was, when and where she was attacked, her injuries and where they were at with the investigation. He then did the same for Robyn.

'So, the guy's good, seems to know his stuff. No trace left on any of the victims at all. Nothing left at the scene. Both victims were caught off guard and they both had ligature marks. We suspect the perp used some sort of cord to strangle the women until they were unconscious. Their heads were covered so they never saw his face.'

'Did he say anything to the victims?' CID officer number one asked as he blew his nose loudly into a cloth handkerchief and stuffed a menthol throat lozenge into his mouth. Great, a stuffy room and snotty germs; I was regretting coming to this meeting.

'Not that the women can recall. We've also deduced that the call made on the victims' phones came from the perp himself. Again, he didn't speak, just left the call to emergency services open. He wanted these women found,' Nick answered.

'If he stayed silent it might be because he's known to the women,' chimed in CID officer number two, voicing what most of us were thinking already. The rapist wouldn't want his voice to be recognised if he knew the victims.

'We've got officers looking at possible suspects. Anyone with a grievance, any sex offenders in the area, any connections between the women,' Jake stated. 'So far, nothing, but it's early days.'

'His choice of victim seems to be random, different age group, different life experiences. These are both good people that help others in a caring capacity, so I guess that could be a possible connection.' CID number one looked pleased with himself.

'Erm, can I ask something?' Shit, I regretted speaking as all eyes turned to face me. If my face wasn't particularly red before, it was definitely a beacon now.

'Of course, Ally, fire away. Ally is helping us to support the women, she's the local counsellor who's been dealing with these cases,' Nick explained to the room of eyes.

'Thanks. It's just, well . . . I've been a counsellor for many years and I've helped many women who have been raped. This is the first time, though, that I've come across anyone who has experienced this level and type of sadistic rape. Y' know, getting stabbed after raped, not murdered. And the calls to emergency services. I mean, how common is this sort of crime?' I knew I was rambling a bit but I hoped they'd understand I wasn't used to this type of case meeting.

'You're right, Ally. It's not common. Sure, there are rapes and stabbings but rarely together, in this manner. These crimes are too organised, too deliberate,' replied Nick.

'So someone this organised, good at covering his tracks . . . surely these women aren't his first victims? I mean, someone this good would have to have developed his level of skill. Y' know, made some earlier mistakes or perfected his technique along the way?' I sat back in my chair and took a long breath in as the eyes that watched me turned to Nick, waiting for his reply.

Nick opened his mouth to speak but CID number two answered instead.

'A good point. I'm presuming, detectives, that

108

you've checked for similar crimes here and in surrounding towns?'

Nick flashed me a 'thanks for making me look like a complete incompetent moron' look and hastily added that officers had checked in Covenston and were now moving to look further afield. Nothing of this level of sadism was standing out. With my face now turning an even deeper red than my sweater, I sat lower in my chair and hoped Nick wouldn't think I was trying to hurt him. I wasn't. I just wanted this nightmare that was sweeping our lovely town to be over already.

The meeting wrapped up fairly quickly, with the CID claiming they were happy with the progress of the investigation so far. They added that they'd get their officers to lend a hand in looking at the database of similar crimes to see if there was any incident that could have been committed by our perp. Maybe evidence of him escalating may turn up. Maybe he'd make a mistake next time. I sighed at all the maybes and slunk out into the cool corridor before Nick could pull me up for my questions.

***

Ally finished off her paperwork, updated the client files, then got changed into her running gear before driving to the cafe to meet Jinny. It was cold and wet but she was too hot and bothered to notice.

'Well, what's up? Spill the beans.' Jinny opened the café door when she saw Ally arrive. A blast of warm air, along with the aroma of garlic, herbs and roasted vegetables, spilled out as she turned to pull the door closed and wave back to Roz.

'It's Nick. I hate him.' Ally pressed the start button on her Garmin as they both fell into pace with each other.

'Really? 'Cause hate wasn't the emotion I got from you when you spoke about him the other day.' Jinny raised her eyebrows to make her point.

'Well, okay, I don't hate him. He just makes me so angry.'

'Sounds like love to me,' Jinny taunted.

'He doesn't want to release certain info to the public and I don't agree.'

'Info about the rapist? Maybe he thinks it might scare him off and then they'll never catch him.'

'Urgh! You think that too. You're supposed to agree with me.'

'No, I'm supposed to listen, be supportive, but also balanced. That's what you do for me.'

'I sat in at a team debrief today. I thought that CID might have prompted him to say more to the media but they're letting Nick lead things and lending support rather than taking over. Which is good for Nick, I suppose.' Ally panted as they ran.

'You're gonna have to take a step back from this, I'd say, or Nick might think you're interfering too much,' Jinny added.

Ally knew she was probably right. 'I know, this whole thing has me rattled. C'mon let's pick up the pace, I need to burn this anger off.'

'Ha, I'll race you.' Jinny laughed, pushing long strides out ahead of Ally.

'Jeez. I didn't mean that fast. I'm not that bloody angry! Slow down.'

***

Jinny

I watched Ally drive off home before I unlocked the

large wooden gate to my garden. I didn't think the customers would appreciate my post-run pong if I nipped through the café to get home while they were eating. The night light came on illuminating the garden. It wasn't dark yet but it was dull enough to activate. It was a bright light, six thousand lumens, they said; could probably see my garden from the moon. And probably a good line of defence considering the rapes. According to the news they had been in public areas, but still, you couldn't be too careful, I thought, as I let myself in and switched off the beeping alarm.

Still too hot from my run to shower, I stuck a homemade lasagne in the microwave to reheat and poured myself a pint of water. I took both to the breakfast bar and popped up my tablet so I could surf while I ate. My phone beeped; Ally letting me know she was home safe so I could relax. At least I wasn't the only one feeling jumpy just now, which prompted me to check twitter for news. The local news tweets were always first to report before radio or TV these days. Thankfully, no new assaults but no apprehension of the rapist either – if it was the same guy. Most of the buzz about the café seemed to think it was, and I had to admit, I did too. I just had a gut feeling about it and my gut was normally right. I was right about Fi, and about Beth - that sense of dread when we discovered her lump. It had happened on many other occasions too. And something about these assaults was scaring me.

I lapped up the last of my lasagne and clicked on Facebook. There was a notification posted on the coven page. I clicked and nearly spat my mouthful of water onto my tablet as a photo flicked up, of Mr. Sleaze holding the missing dog, Benji.

'No fucking way,' I yelled and my phone pinged

at the swearing.

The post said, Only two hours after the spell Simon was walking home and found Benji in the park across the road from where he and his neighbours live. Simon said his neighbours were delighted at Benji's return and offered him the £800 reward. Simon gracefully told them to donate the award to a charity of their choice. We, at the coven, are delighted the spell worked so quickly and Benji was found safe and well.

I hit the Facetime to Ally.

'What?' A wet towel-turbaned face filled my screen.

'Did you check out the coven Facebook page?'

'Not had a chance this week. Too busy.'

'Have a look.'

'Now?'

'Yeah, go on. It'll take you a mo.' My connection said it was paused as Ally flipped apps. Her eyes were wide when she came back on screen.

'No fucking way,' she yelled. My phone vibrated as I'm sure hers did too.

'I bet he fucking (vibrate) stole the dog and produced it conveniently after the spell.' My gut told me I was right. Either that, or it was telling me my lasagne had hit the spot.

'He did! I know it. That wasn't a dog missing for days. Did you see how clean it was? There's no way that dog was in that park since it got lost.'

'I agree. I just hate to say this, but I really don't blo– like Simon.' I watched the ceiling as Ally talked while she dried off and dressed somewhere off-screen.

'I don't like him either. Tomorrow, I think I'll ask him how the dog was so clean.'

'Do. I'd love to hear his excuse.'

'I guess you're still sitting in your running gear? Aren't you sweaty? I had to shower right away.'

'Was still sweating and too hungry. You had time to cool off on the drive home. I don't see anything else on there. So I'll pick you up tomorrow.'

'Bye,' Ally ended the feed before I could reply. I stuck my nose into my armpit. Ally was right, I was stinking. Definitely time for a shower now.

***

As they walked into the Bamras' drawing room, Ally and Jinny both clocked the bottle of Champagne chilling in the middle of the buffet table. Jinny tried not to laugh as Ally rolled her eyes. The room was buzzing and Simon was holding court, boasting about how he 'just felt drawn to the park' and how a whining led him deeper in to find poor Benji cowering under a bush. Jinny put her hand on Ally's arm, feeling her ready to rush forward and question him. As Ally caught her eye, she mouthed, 'Later,' and was graced with another eye roll – although a more prolonged one this time. Luckily, her back was to Debbie, who was heading towards them with a glass of something sparkly.

'No booze for me,' Jinny got in quickly. 'I'm the chauffeur.'

'It's just sparkling grape juice,' Debbie reassured them. 'No alcohol till after the spell casting.'

By now Ally had pasted a smile on her face, a genuine one Jinny noted.

'Then yes, please,' Ally said, thanking her.

'Go on then.' Jinny took the other glass.

'Isn't it great news?' Debbie beamed at them both. 'I was so worried about that little dog, I had planned to gather up some people and go and join the searches for him. Do you think our spell could've really brought him out?'

'Oh, without a doubt,' Ally said.

Jinny heard the sarcasm that Debbie obviously hadn't as she was still beaming from ear to ear and clapping her hands like a four-year-old with a new toy. Jinny nudged Ally, Ally gave her an innocent 'What?' look. Jinny just raised her brow in return and watched Ally look away, trying not to laugh.

'So what spells are we doing tonight?' Jinny asked Debbie.

'I don't know yet. There wasn't anything mentioned on the agenda apart from Simon's success. But I think we're about to find out . . .' Debbie pointed as Nasir and Amira waved everyone into a circle.

Amira led the session, and Jinny couldn't help her eyes be drawn to Simon. He was glowing from the praise Amira gave him and appeared disappointed when the conversation moved from him on to the night's agenda. She had no doubt in her mind that Simon had engineered the whole thing, from stealing the dog before the last coven meeting, to asking for the spell and to recovering the poor thing. He just loved himself, Jinny thought, from the circle, her super skinny, designer jeans not the best clothing for sitting cross-legged. He was looking around the group to see who was looking at him. Jinny quickly dropped her eyes before he got to her, but still she shivered a little as she felt his stare. She looked up to where Charley was sitting between Amira and Debbie, smiling when she caught her eye. Charley gave her a warm smile back and a silent, 'Hi.' Jinny winked and watched her cheeks redden slightly as her smile widened. Ally nudged Jinny and she realised she was missing what was being said.

'. . . So we thought it would be good to cast a protection spell on the town first. How does that sound?' Amira looked around the circle for approval. The group were all nodding their heads in agreement.

'And then after that, does anyone have any suggestions as to what else they'd like to do?' Amira looked around the room. Debbie put her hand up. 'Debbie? You got a suggestion?'

'Well, most of us here have been members for a while and we have our familiars. So I thought it would be a good idea to do a spell to help the three latest newcomers find their familiars?'

'Oh my God, I think I'm going to laugh uncontrollably,' Ally whispered in Jinny's ear.

Jinny took a deep breath and tried to keep her face straight as she whispered back, 'Don't you fucking dare!'

'It'd just be my luck a fucking giant spider would turn out to be mine.'

Jinny struggled not to laugh. Ally was as near an arachnophobe as you could get, and none of her psychotherapy training ever got her over it.

'And I'd have a swarm of bloody bloodthirsty horseflies following me everywhere.' Ally's fear of spiders almost equated to Jinny's disgust of horseflies.

They looked at each other with tears in their eyes, stifling their laughter. Jinny's cheeks burned holding them stiff. She caught Charley sending her a questioning shrug. 'Later,' Jinny mouthed as a tear leaked down her cheek. She felt Ally's arm shaking next to her in silent hysterics. Jinny moved slightly away so she could try to regain some control. Luckily, everyone else had their eyes now closed as Amira started the relaxation meditation and protection spell. Everyone except Simon, who was staring at her.

He winked as she caught his eye. That soon sobered Jinny up as she just raised her eyebrows at him and closed her eyes. His creepy, smug face was imprinted on her eyelids as it faded to a red silhouette under her lids.

Meditations and spells over with, Champagne was now being poured for those not driving. Jinny watched Ally sip some while talking to Nasir, when Simon accosted her. He was staring at her open blouse while he spoke to her.

'So Jinny, how're you enjoying the group?' Still no eye contact.

'So far I find it interesting. How long have you been a member?' Simon looked up and wriggled his eyebrows up and down.

'I've been a *member*,' he emphasised with more eyebrow action, 'for two years now.'

Jinny intended to ignore his innuendoes. He may be considered good-looking but he creeped her out. She wondered if he was the rapist. 'You work out at the local gym?'

'I do,' he said puffing his chest out. 'I'm there five nights a week.'

'Were you there that night of the attack?'

'I was. Terrible thing. I left before it happened and when I heard about it I tried to think if I'd seen anyone suspicious hanging about in the car park, but I didn't. It was deserted.'

'I heard they're putting up more cameras now.'

'And more lights. The back of the car park was always dark and beside the woods, anyone could've been lurking there. You go to the gym?' He was now giving her the once over.

'Not often. I prefer running, but I was a purple belt in karate. So I think I can handle myself,' Jinny added, in case he *was* the rapist.

'Cool. Oh there's Debbie. I wanted a word with her . . .' he headed off quickly.

Well, he obviously doesn't like strong women.

Jinny helped herself to more grape juice and headed over to Charley, who was eyeing up the mini desserts. Jinny had been informed by Amira that everything was vegan, and gluten and nut free on the table and should be safe for everyone to eat. She lifted a raw cacao truffle from under Charley's fingers.

'They are so good,' Charley said, helping herself to another two. 'I've already had two.'

'Mmm, they are,' Jinny agreed, noting to herself to ask Amira for the recipe. 'These'd go down well in the café.'

'Oh they would. And I'd never leave.' She giggled.

'I can't see me complaining about that,' Jinny flirted, watching Charley blush.

Charley nudged her playfully. 'So, what were you two laughing at?'

'We were thinking of our worst possible familiars and it just got out of hand. What would your worst be?'

'I'm not sure. I suppose it would be something ridiculous – like an elephant or something.' She laughed and Jinny joined in.

'Oh God, don't get me started again. So have you got a familiar already?'

'Nope not yet. And this is the first time it was mentioned at the coven, so I hadn't even given it a thought. What's a familiar for, anyway?'

'Your guess is as good as mine. I'll be sure to look it up when I get home. The only thing I know about them is from horror movies. And usually the familiar was either suckling at mysteriously formed third nipples or being killed as a blood sacrifice for the spell to work.'

'Gruesome. Maybe I'll look it up too. I think I should've done that before I joined in the spell.' Charley giggled some more. She pointed to Nasir's cat as it followed him about. 'But I would love a cat, but knowing my luck I'd end up with a lion.'

Ally sidled up to them as they were still laughing. 'Right, there's too much hilarity here. You wouldn't catch me making fun of this stuff.' Her poker face twitched to crack.

Jinny brushed off Ally's shoulder. 'Is that a spider I see?' Ally squealed then laughed, punching Jinny in the shoulder.

'Bitch.'

'You two are crazy.' Charley shook her head. 'But I don't think I've had so much fun at this until you two started. Please keep coming.'

'Oh, I will,' Jinny promised and looked at Ally expectantly.

'We'll see,' was all she offered. 'Are you ready to head? I want to get to bed early tonight and up for a run in the morning. You joining me?' She looked at Jinny.

'What? For a run? Sure.'

'Right, well come on. Nice seeing you again, Charley. You still getting a lift home?'

'Yes, thanks. And it was great seeing you both.' She turned to Jinny. 'Maybe see you next week? I thought I'd come to the café one day for lunch.'

'I'm there every day. So anytime that suits you.'

'Great. I'll check my diary and text you.'

'Magic! No pun intended,' Jinny said as Ally sighed and dragged her away.

The ride took them through town to get to Ally's neck of the woods. Like any Saturday night, the centre was crowded with teens and young adults in various states of disrepair and inebriation. While waiting for the lights to change, Ally and Jinny watched as five young girls fell about outside a club.

'Oh no,' Ally fumed. 'Look at them. It's only half nine and those three in particular can hardly stand.'

Jinny shook her head. 'They've probably been drinking all day.'

'I must be getting old. I feel worried for them, especially with those rapes. You feel invincible at that age. I guess they're not even giving it a thought.'

The lights changed and Jinny drove off as Ally watched the girls drag their friends over to the bus stop.

'I'm going to nag Nick some more. See if he'll put some more police out on the beat and maybe get reporters to warn people to be more careful when out at night.'

'To be honest, it's all I hear people talk about, Ally. So you can't save everyone. Or change their behaviour. As infuriating as that is, there's nothing we can do about it.'

'But Jinny, if you saw what those poor women went through . . . He doesn't just rape them. I shouldn't be telling you this, so please don't let anyone know–'

'I won't.'

'Those women were tied up, choked and raped. He's a sick bastard.'

'The news said they were stabbed too.'

'Yes, but it isn't random, Jinny. This guy knows what he's doing. The stab wounds are directed at the uterus. We think he's making sure these women don't have kids.'

'Fuck's sake.' Both their phones vibrated. 'There was nothing about that on the news.'

'Exactly! That's why I think Nick should be getting this information out there. It's not enough to say there's a rape and stabbing. There's motive behind this psychopath's behaviour.'

'Why? Why rape and then destroy chances of having kids? Is he afraid he makes them pregnant?'

'No. He wears a condom. There's no trace of his DNA. And we suspect he doesn't want to kill them either because he phones for an ambulance.'

'Jeez, that's scary.'

'I know.'

'You know, Sleazy Simon was at the gym the same night as the first attack. Said he left before it happened.'

Ally looked at Jinny, whose eyes remained on the road. 'Do you think he–'

'Ally, he creeps me out big time. But when I told him I did karate he buggered off like I'd farted in his face. So maybe he doesn't like strong women.'

'Yeah, I noticed he tries to corner Charley a lot.'

'I saw that too, last week. I'll bloody make sure he doesn't in future.'

'I'll mention to Nick about him being at the gym. But I suppose I can't accuse all sleazebags as suspects.'

'The other girl wasn't attacked at the gym, but I did wonder if she was a gym member.'

'Good point. I'll ask her next time I'm counselling her.'

'Listen to us, armchair detectives.' Jinny laughed, lightening the mood as they drove up to Ally's cottage.

'You sure you don't want to stay at mine tonight?' Jinny offered.

'Nah, I'll get to bed early and read. I'll see you in the morning.'

'Okay. I'll watch till you're in.'

'Okay. Text me when you're home.'

'Will do.'

Ally let herself in and watched Jinny drive off before putting the large bolt across the door. Even that didn't make her feel safe just now.

***

Jinny

I woke with a start at the outside light flooding my room and a noise of rustling from the garden.

Shit. Someone's in my bloody garden.

I jumped out of bed, my heart racing and quickly threw on my sweatpants and T-shirt. The floodlight went out and it took a moment for my eyes to adjust to the shadows of trees in the garden. It was a still night, so I knew the rustling wasn't the wind. I waited. There it was again. My heart leapt a few more beats.

Shit, was someone down there?

I heard it again. Someone *was* in my garden.

Should I call the police?

I grabbed my phone from its charger, the screen light illuminating my face. A branch from the tree hit my window and I dropped the phone.

Jeez I nearly shit myself there, I bent down to pick it up, hoping it wasn't broken. As the outside light came back on a pair of green eyes met mine. I screamed – and then laughed when I saw it was a cat. Stuck up in my tree, no doubt. I opened the window and leaned out to try to grab it. It yowled at me, slinking further into the trunk. Dammit. I was going to have to try enticing it down. The more I reached out, the further back it went.

I grabbed my fleece, stuck my feet into my trainers and went down the stairs to the kitchen door and out to the garden. It was bloody cold, but I was going to get that damn cat down whether it wanted to come or not. I looked about the brightly-lit garden, reassured no one else was there. Fishing around my garbage, I found the lasagne carton from earlier. Hopefully, the cat wouldn't mind fake mincemeat, I thought, as I waved it about under the tree.

'Here kitty, kitty. Come on. Come get some dinner.'

It just yowled some more at me. Shit. The tree looked sturdy enough. I'd climbed it before, when I was trying to stick a birdhouse in it, and although I hadn't gone up that high, it was doable. The branches caught my hair so I twirled it into a knot at the top of my head and started climbing. It wasn't hard. When I got to the branch right below the cat I was able to stand, balanced out on the limb, with one hand holding the higher branch that the cat was on. With my free hand I pulled the lasagne carton out my pocket and offered it up. The cat was all black except for a white tuft on its neckline that looked like a bowtie. It was as scrawny as hell, too.

As it gingerly came towards the carton, I realised I hadn't really thought this out very well, had I? How the hell was I going to get the cat down? I started pulling the carton towards me, to entice it down. It just looked at me and cried some more. I put the carton on the branch, wedging it into finer branch divisions, allowing my free hand to try to grab the cat. Nearly there. I reached out and the little bastard swiped at my hand. I pulled back in fright when the branch I was standing on snapped. It felt like I was moving in slow motion as I crashed down the tree, arse first, bouncing off a few branches as I hit the ground. I looked up. I couldn't see the cat now. Damn. I was going to have to call the fire station.

I stood up, nearly impaling myself on the shard of a branch sticking out – although grateful the larger part of it, now on the ground, had cushioned my landing. I went upstairs to my room to get my phone and there was the little bugger, licking itself clean on my bed. I bent down apprehensively to pet it. I didn't want to get swiped again; there was a red welt already forming on the back of my hand. This time though it purred, rolling onto its back exposing a loose, flabby tummy with lots of little nipples.

This girl has just had kittens.

She nudged her head against my hand, now purring loudly. Then she bounced off the bed and ran out the door. I followed her to find her crying at the back door so I let her out but she just stood looking at me. She moved a few feet away and, meowing loudly, turned to look back at me. Did she want me to follow her?

'What the hell do you want, I'm not a bloody cat whisperer you know.' She moved another couple of feet away and waited. I moved up to her as she went over to the bush under the tree and meowed some more.

'This is getting ridiculous,' I said to the cat as I bent down to pick her up but she pulled back into the bush. Moving the bush aside, I saw what all the fuss was about. Six little eyes staring up at me. Bloody hell, three kittens. What the hell was I going to do now?

***

Jinny answered the door to Ally, still in her sweat pants and running top.

'Aren't you ready yet?' Ally breezed in passed her, leaving her Garmin on the windowsill to get a GPS signal. 'That tree out there's got a broken branch. Nearly tore my top.'

'Yeah, I'll deal with that later.' Jinny pulled Ally into the kitchen. 'We have a problem, Houston.' Jinny pointed to the corner of the kitchen. 'Meet Mrs Tux and her babies.'

Ally's eyes widened as she dived to the cat bed Jinny had made from a cardboard box and an old sweatshirt. 'Aw, where did you get them?' she crooned.

'Long story short, I found them under the bush in the garden. By the looks of it she's been there a few weeks, probably living off café titbits.'

'They're adorable.'

'Oh fuck!' Jinny looked up, eyes wide.

'What? What's wrong?' Ally looked at the cats, then back to Jinny, confused.

Jinny rushed down to the floor beside her. 'What? Oh . . . Nothing's wrong with the cats, but I'm a bit freaked about this. Aren't you?'

'Freaked about what? They're adorable.' Ally lifted out one of the kittens, gave it to Jinny and took one for herself.

'No. I mean, yes, they are adorable.' Jinny nuzzled into her little bundle. 'But – the spell?'

'What sp– Oh.' Ally realised what Jinny meant. 'Shit, how many of us needed familiars?'

'Me, you and Charley. And Charley even said to me she would love a cat.'

'Well, there are four cats here, so maybe it's just a coincidence.'

'Ally, this is not a coincidence. The very night we do the spell, I find more than enough familiars for all of us. That's not a coincidence.'

124

Ally shook her head. 'I don't believe for one minute it was the spell. If there'd been three I might've wondered, but four? Nah. We both think Simon faked it. So that wasn't the spell. And we also put out a spell to protect the town from the rapist. I can't see that happening, can you?'

'You never know . . .'

Ally gave Jinny one of her 'don't give me that shit' looks.

'Well, anyway. What am I going to do with this lot?'

Ally smiled at Jinny and took out her phone. 'Hi Nirja, I hope I didn't disturb you, but my sister just found a cat and her nursing kittens. Can you advise us?' Ally listened and ah-hah'd a few times, then ended the call. She texted something into the phone and looked up, smiling.

'Who was that?'

'Vet nurse pal of mine. Said she'll come over in an hour or so and scan the cat. I texted her your address. I told her to come through the café so she doesn't spear herself on that broken branch out there. She'll bring stuff to tide you over for a bit to look after them while mummy nurses. If the cat has an owner she'll follow that up and if the owner wants the kittens then you'll have to hand them over, but if they don't, then they will need to be homed.'

'Wow! Well done you. Ally, you do realise if there is an owner who wants her cat but not the kittens, then the spell could very well have worked.'

'I think you're grasping at straws there, sis.'

'We'll see . . .'

125

CHAPTER NINE

You'd normally not perform again so soon after your last fix, but it'll all fit together nicely. You can't be stopped from doing your work. You need to do it. This one's ideal. People are so fucking stupid these days, their whole lives on social media. Information like bread crumbs, leaving trails all over the place. Where they live, where they work. It just takes some fishing around, maybe an email or two, and the plan is in place. The stupid cunts are so naïve, they have no clue they've been complicit in their own fix.

At least it didn't take you too long to work out the best place. This spot is perfect. Out of town. Away from all of the prying, suspicious eyes. There's no heat here. You can take your time, all the delicious time in the world, and still get back to see the latest episode of that show you've been watching.

Finally, your prey has arrived. You can see her car's headlights making their way along the empty road. You had to park at the shopping centre, among all the other cars doing early evening shopping or seeing movies, and walk ten minutes along the fence line to the warehouse park in the next town over. You couldn't have her seeing your car, not when the place is so deserted. It's ideal, and pretty smart of you to make sure you were seen going into the cinema hall earlier at the shopping centre. They'd not notice you coming back out with a blonde wig and plain cap on. Two nights ago you cut the video surveillance wire to the warehouse here. No one's been here since last week, so no footage to worry about. Preparation is everything. Best laid plans have better outcomes. That's what your mother would say. She always ran an efficient house.

The bitch comes here every Sunday for a stock-take. All it took was a call to her store, some questions and a few minutes work on the internet and hey-fucking-presto all you need to know to set up your plan. You've waited for an hour. Not long now and you'll be able to get out from behind this stinking garbage container. The smell is repugnant to you but intoxicating to all the bloody flies swarming around. The waiting gives you time. Checking your plan over, thinking. Your parents would be proud of you. They taught you well. They taught you right from wrong. Father's beatings were hard, but you deserved them; it was for your own good. Sometimes, the belt cut through your skin. As she cleaned your wounds, Mother said Father knew what he was doing, it would teach you. They loved you. It was hard love, but they loved you, even when you were bad.

You're ready now. She's ready now, for her fix. You like to watch them for a few moments before you start the process. Watch them being oblivious to what's about to happen. Unsuspecting, weak in her current, unfixed state she's humming loudly to the song that was just playing on her car radio as she grabs the clipboard from the back seat and goes into the warehouse. She sounds happy. You can make her really happy.

She's singing now, some pop song about being saved, and has no fucking idea how apt those words are as she comes back out of the warehouse, her arms loaded up with materials and sewing threads for her haberdashery business. You watch her as you slink behind her, shadowing her moves. This is one of your easier fixes. The game, *your* game feels good. You watch as she balances on one foot. Her other foot pushes further open the back door of her car that she left slightly open for convenience and she bends in to lay the stuff on the back seat. Like a panther you pounce.

Getting the hood on is easy and you use your knee on her lower back to restrain her as she flails about, her hands trying to loosen the tightening cord of the hood. As she passes out you pull up her corduroy mini skirt. It's more like a fucking belt than a skirt. The cunt has no shame or morals. Another lesson you can teach her. With her tights down round her knees, you thrust into her hard; she needs to wake now. You need her awake to feel the pleasure of the fix. Her face is pushed among the materials on the back seat and as she stirs, you get to enjoy the muffled groans and whimpers. You grunt loudly as you come, thrusting more slowly now, relishing the change you are creating. You don't need to be quiet or fast out here.

She's lying so still, like a hypnotised rabbit, as you turn her to complete the fix with the Buck knife from your back pocket. Father's knife. He'd be glad you put it to good use now. You'll never forget the disappointment on his face when he thrust its walnut handle in your palm and told you to kill the young hare he'd snared in the field. But you can forget that now. It's not important, not like this. Your father would be proud now. Proud of your work and proud that you have found your way with his knife. You keep the blade sharp so it slides through the delicate skin above her pubic bone. Just like cutting into a tender steak.

You know she'll pass out soon. They always do. Then you can clear your stuff from the scene. Your kit. All disposable: gloves, cable ties, non-fibrous cloth for gag, suit, condom. You'll burn them later. You don't take a trophy. Your trophy will be seeing those you fixed. You have to be careful. Once checked, you use her thumb to unlock her phone and dial emergency services. You can score off this latest addition to the list.

CHAPTER TEN

Ally

I was sobbing, deep heart-wrenching sobs, as the water from the shower fell onto my head and back. The meltdown started not long after Nick called with news of another rape. He sounded stressed, desperate, even. I wasn't to hurry in, as the poor woman would be in theatre for a while. Same MO. I'd decided to take a shower to wake myself up – it was quarter to midnight on a Sunday night. Maybe Steph could cover my clients tomorrow. I was exhausted. I tried to think of anything other than the horrors that would await me at the hospital, but as soon as the water hit my body, I slithered to the shower floor, hugging my legs as tears and water mingled. It was too much. How much longer could I do this? If this mental exhaustion continued, I could see myself needing counselling; everyone's pain bearing down on me and I felt responsible even though I knew I wasn't. I guess I cared too much.

Feeling somewhat better after my 'release', and confirming that Steph could do my shift, I headed to the forensics tent that Nick said he'd be in for the next few hours. I wanted a full update, I wanted to help find this creep, help to make things safe again, for women, for the town.

I set my satnav to find the warehouse park, I hated driving to somewhere I didn't know in the dark. The area was outside of Covenston and was very industrialised, so there was no need for me to ever be there. Turning the corner on the satnav's instruction I knew exactly where to go as soon as I spotted the throng of reporters outside the entrance to the park. How did they get there so fast? It was the early hours of Monday morning, for Christ's sake. They looked hungry for news and the word 'serial' was being used in every news report I tuned in to. Nick would be getting hammered if he didn't feed the lions. He needed to use the press to his advantage because he was coming up empty on the forensics side. So many complicated cases are solved when a witness reports something that they feel is out of place, and this was proving complicated.

There were several police vehicles and two large tents set up, one over the actual scene and another for the staff. A policewoman at the staff tent let me through. I'd never been this close to a crime scene before, and I could feel some eyes on me, no doubt wondering why a civilian was wandering about. I couldn't see Nick, but Jake was there.

'Jake, Nick told me to come here first for an update before I headed to the hospital. Is he around?'

'No. Well, yeah, he's around, but he's busy. He asked me to update you. Said he'll try catch up with you later.'

'Oh. Okay, yeah. That's fine.' I tried not to sound disappointed but the smirk on Jake's face told me I was rumbled. God, the guy irritated me. I could feel my cheeks burning and I tried to distract him with a question. 'So, what do I need to know? Who's the victim this time?'

'It's one of the gay women that was on the news the other day. Y' know the couple that got thrown out of their own wedding reception? Denise Whitelaw.'

'Oh my God, really?'

'Yep. Same MO, to the letter. Raped, stabbed, marks on her neck and the call made from her phone.'

'And forensics? I know it's too early but–'

'Too early, but this guy's good. They're going through everything now but I doubt we'll find anything; he seems to really know what he's doing. Maybe we'll get lucky and he made a mistake.' He nodded in the direction of the other forensic tent. 'Nick's over there now.'

'Please tell me he's going to tell the reporters more? They're all saying it's a serial, anyway.'

'It'll be me talking to them. I'm heading out now. And yes,' Jake held his hand up just as I was about to interrupt, 'I will be saying it looks like it's the same guy. I'll also be telling them that we'll be appealing to the public following a reconstruction of Gill's case. It'll be broadcast on Tuesday and–' He held up his hand again as my mouth opened. This guy was definitely annoying. 'We'll be asking the public if they've seen anything suspicious on all dates.'

'Good,' was all that I could manage. I felt relieved they would give the public more information. 'Jake, have you found any connections yet . . . between the victims?'

'Nothing. We've checked phone records, places the women frequent, friends. Nada. It looks random.'

'This is a hate crime . . .yeah? Against women.'

'Yeah, but we can't protect every woman, if he's picking them off randomly.' Jake sounded rattled.

'Denise Whitelaw was gay. Maybe the creep

saw her at the demo. Could it be because she's a strong woman? Gill was always vocal about women's rights.'

'It could be. But where does that leave us with Robyn?'

'I know. I'm sorry, I'm just thinking out loud. Bill Bishopton . . . What about him?'

'Look, Bishopton's name is on our list for questioning. Ally, we're doing everything we can just now. There's a process.'

'What? So we've just got to wait around until one by one we're picked off?' I could feel my emotions start to spin.

'Ally, we can't just pull every male in this town in for questioning. Anyone that looks suspect will be called in, I can assure you. Nick's spoken to the victim's partner and family. They're expecting you at the hospital. He let the staff know you've been called in.'

'Okay. Yeah . . . I'll go there now. Thanks, Jake.' I turned to leave. I'd hoped Nick might appear before I left, but there was no sign of him. I hadn't seen him since the debrief and I wanted to find out if he was pissed off with me.

'By the way, Nick said to tell you hi. Said sorry for not being available.' Jake smirked again. He knew I fancied Nick; I really needed to learn how to hide my feelings more.

***

The hospital had even more reporters hanging about outside, with television crews using the hospital sign as their backdrop, and the police were screening all visitors as they entered. I met Jan, one of the liaison policewomen that had looked after Gill's family, on my way through the car park, and we walked in together. I was hoping for some new information but she had none, except that Denise's family were devastated and worried that her partner Karen, who was four months pregnant, might miscarry again – she had lost the baby at five months last time.

The high dependency doors opened automatically as we arrived and I noticed that the relatives' room was crowded with anxious-looking family members from various generations. Denise's room was opposite the nurses' station and I guessed it was Karen who sat next to Denise, her head resting on the mattress as she held her hand. I wondered fleetingly if Jinny knew the couple from any gay events or the active gay community groups.

Denise looked pretty out of it still. Her face had sustained some bruising around her eye and a small cut on her cheekbone. She was very beautiful; dark ebony skin, full lips and high cheekbones. She looked peaceful now, but that was simply due to the cocktail of drugs she'd have been given in surgery. In the corridor, I stopped the nurse who had just changed one of Denise's intravenous bags.

'Hi, I'm Allison Canessa, the counsellor. I think DCI Daniels told the family to expect me?'

'Oh, yeah. I spoke to the Inspector Daniels earlier when he came in to see Denise, but she was still in recovery. He mentioned you'd be by. The family don't want anyone in just now, though.'

'What? Why? I'm only here to help.'

'I know, but they insisted. When the liaison policewoman tried to speak with Denise earlier, just after surgery, she became pretty hysterical. We had to sedate her or she was just going to injure herself.'

'I see. And the family? Can I speak with them?'

'I'm sorry. They were pretty clear that they

only want to deal with the police and liaison just now. I think they're all pretty freaked out by everything. First, with what happened at their wedding, then the demo, and now this.'

'Okay, I get it. Can you give them my card at least, just in case?'

The nurse smiled sympathetically and nodded as she took my card. I couldn't blame the family. It was normal to close ranks to outsiders when tragedy occurred.

'They don't want me there,' I said despondently to Jan who was now heading into the patient's room.

'That's how it is with some families. Lots of them even hate *us* being there. It's not personal.'

'I know. I'd just hoped that maybe I could help.'

'Ally, I'll be here, and if there's any further information I'm sure DCI Daniels will pass it on. We'll get there, don't worry.'

'Jan, can you let her partner know I'm also available to her to talk if she needs me? It might help take some of the stress away. Stress is not good for unstable pregnancies.'

'I will tell her, Ally. That's a good idea. They might even want to be counselled together.'

'Thanks, Jan.'

There wasn't much point in remaining at the hospital so I headed back home for a couple of hours to grab some sleep, which turned out to be pointless as my head was buzzing. I tried anyway, dozing on and off. At midday I went into the centre, even though Steph was covering my appointments. There's always paperwork to do, something I had neglected recently with the rapes.

Sharon stuck her head through the door. 'You okay, honey? Can I get you a coffee or lunch from the café?'

'You know, Sharon, that'd be great.' I closed over the file, glad of the distraction. 'Will you get me my usual? And I'll answer the phone while you're away.'

'Of course. But you'd better get your butt in here because it's ringing already.'

I could hear Sharon exchange hellos on her way out and when I looked up from the call Nick was perched on the back of a seat waiting on me to finish. Could he look any more gorgeous with that floppy fringe and half smile? As I placed the handset down, I felt myself become self-conscious under his watchful eye.

'Nick, hi. I . . . I didn't expect you.'

'Well, you weren't at the hospital and Jan told me what happened.'

'Yeah. I'm sorry. I'd hoped–'

'Sorry? What for? If that's what the family want . . .' He shrugged. 'Look, I came by to let you know that we've spoken to Bill Bishopton on the grounds that he threatened Denise at the demo. He has an alibi. His wife, Anne, says he was at home. She said he's barely left home since he was cautioned.'

'Do you believe her? He's the only one so far with a reason to hurt someone.'

'He has no connection to the other women, though.'

'But he does know Gill. Debbie said she'd reported him to the police after he last beat Anne up.'

'And Robyn? Ally, if he has an alibi, all we can do is keep an eye on him and question the victims about possible motives.'

'I know. I'm sorry. I hate this. I feel so helpless.' I was surprised at my own admission. Nick moved closer to me, taking advantage of it. Was it an invitation? I wasn't sure, but I moved closer to him as well. I wanted to feel his arms around me, to feel protected. That wasn't like me; I hesitated, unsure of my own actions.

Sharon breezed in. 'I'm back . . . Oh. Not interrupting anything, I hope?'

I felt like a teenager getting caught about to kiss my boyfriend by a parent.

'Actually,' Nick said, 'I was just about to tell Ally about a self-defence class at the community centre. It'll start on Thursday. I asked Ken, one of my martial arts buddies, to take the class. He's taught both women and men self-defence in the past and he can do a short course. To help folk feel a bit safer. What d'you think?'

'That's a great idea, Nick,' I agreed, putting a little distance between us again.

'Oh, it was Reverend Proctor's idea. I just set the wheels in motion. He thought it might help, and yeah . . . it's a good idea.'

'Thanks for getting that organised. I'll let folk know.'

We said our goodbyes, letting our eyes connect for longer than necessary. I couldn't wait to tell Jinny.

***

Jinny

Having kittens to look after was highly restricting to my fitness regime, so when Linda offered to look after them for a couple of hours I leapt at the chance. A run to the gym, a session on the weights and a run back would make up for my lack of exercise this past week.

I was busy adding on another half a kilo to each side of the barbell when the smell of heavy sweat assaulted my nose and a hand slide around my waist. I jumped back, turning to see sleazy Simon letching at my cleavage – again.

'Hey, thought that was you. I'd recognise those legs anywhere,' he leered, giving me a slow look up and down.

I felt naked and exposed. 'Simon, didn't anyone tell you it's sexual harassment to touch someone up without–'

'Hey, hey, I didn't mean anything.' He pulled his hands away quickly, holding them up in the air.

'Do it again and you'll be kissing the deck.'

'What's got you all worked up, eh? Can't a friend say hello?' He looked furious, but I would not be groped by anyone, whether I knew them or not. I told him so.

'Must be PMS, eh?'

I was ready to deck him. Sexist prick. Before I could respond, he waved over to some girl, who also looked like she wanted the ground to swallow her up, and made his way over to her.

I worked my anger off on the weights and was feeling altogether stress-free when I exited the gym and sorted my backpack out for the run home. At least it was still light. I was about to start my timer when I heard a raised voice tell someone to leave her alone. Of course, it was Simon, now harassing the same girl I saw him escape to after our little debacle. I couldn't ignore it. My heart was racing and I could feel my legs weaken with adrenaline, but I really *couldn't* ignore it. He had her backed up against her car, one hand either side of her on the car roof, virtually trapping her, and from what I could see his pelvis was pressing into her. Her face was red and I could hear her try to get out of the situation.

'I . . . I'm meeting my boyfriend . . . I . . .'

'What's going on here?' I belted out as I approached.

He dropped his hands away from the girl and stood back. 'Hey, Jinny. Still worked up I see.'

'Still harassing women, I see.'

'You got it all wrong. Susie and I go way back. Don't we, Susie?'

Susie looked guilty, but still uncomfortable. 'Yeah. But I have to go.' She quickly opened her car door and got in.

'Bye, Susie. Maybe next time,' Simon called after her reversing car.

I felt vulnerable in the diminishing light, alone with him in the car park. I looked up at the newly-installed security cameras.

He followed my eyes and coyly smiled. 'Well, see you at the coven. Hope you're in a better mood,' he called back to me as he jogged off to his car.

I was fuming. I was seriously considering talking to the other coven members and asking if they would consider banning him. Or was it just me he harassed? Maybe I should ask the others first. I ran home, now almost dark, keeping to the busy main roads instead of the unlit off-road paths. My legs felt shaky after the car park scenario but I had to push them the three miles homeward. And of course, it would start raining half way home. Just wasn't my day.

***

'I think I've got a crush on Inspector Gorgeous,' Ally admitted, sitting on Jinny's kitchen floor, cuddling the only all-black kitten. 'I thought he was going to kiss me the other day. Although maybe I imagined it.'

Jinny put a cup of coffee for Ally on the

breakfast bar and sipped her own, resisting the urge to disturb the other sleeping kittens for a cuddle. They looked so contented, snuggled up to their mum. 'Why? What happened?'

Ally put the sleeping kitten back with the others and rose to claim her coffee. She took a drink. 'We were talking and he came right up to me. Honestly, if Sharon hadn't chosen that minute to come back, I'm positive he would've even just cuddled me. I think he could sense I was feeling quite down at that point.'

'Sounds promising. If he was going to make a move on you and was interrupted then he will try again.'

'I hope so. Maybe I should make a move, let him know I'm interested?'

'Why not? It's about time you moved on. After all, there hasn't been anyone since Anthony. It's time you got back in the game . . . and the sack.'

Ally sighed and drank her coffee. Jinny couldn't offer more advice than that. Especially since she was thinking about Charley, too.

Ally broke into her thoughts with a change of subject. 'So, what did Nirja say about the cats?'

'Well, mummy cat is chipped. Nirja contacted the owner who was delighted to hear her cat had been found, but not so happy about the kittens. Nirja told her I'd take them if she would let me keep mummy cat for a couple of weeks till they were weaned. Turns out the woman was going off on holiday for two weeks, so it was perfect, really.'

'That's great news. I presume one is mine, then? Can I have dibs on the all black cute one?'

'She's all yours. I'll let Charley decide on what one she wants and I'll keep the last. You do realise that means we now have one cat for each person that needed a familiar?'

'Jinny it's just a coincidence. Honestly.'

'Hmm, I'm not so sure.' Jinny finished her coffee and put her coat on ready to leave for the coven meeting. 'The evidence for them is outweighing the evidence against them, if you ask me.'

Ally rinsed her cup out and grabbed her jacket and bag and followed Jinny out to the car. 'No way. Every incident can be explained rationally.' She got in the car and continued her case. 'For example, your spell about getting rid of Kevin, didn't get rid of him alone. And you did suspect Fiona's relationship with Kevin was a bit off even before you did it.'

'Yeah, but–'

'Hear me out,' Ally insisted as Jinny kept her eyes on the road. 'We both agreed that Simon did not find that dog.'

'I agree he probably rigged that one but–'

'Ah, ah, not finished. The cat and her kittens were not the exact number for everyone that needed a familiar.'

'But it is in the end.'

'An easy coincidence. I'm still not buying it.'

'The other spell we did at the coven also asked to protect the town from the rapist. And the last rape wasn't in town, Ally.'

'Yeah but Denise was from town. So I'd call bullshit on that.'

Jinny laughed. She knew she wouldn't win with Ally. And she was right. There was nothing that couldn't be explained away as coincidence.

'Listen, talking about Simon, I had a run in with him at the gym the other day.'

'Why? What happened? Why're you just telling me now?'

'When I got back I was distracted trying to save

141

my sofa from acrobatic shearing kittens. And then I got tied up with work.'

'What happened?'

Ally sat staring at her open-mouthed as Jinny explained. 'Holy, fuck!' Ally cried as both their phones buzzed. 'Sorry, but I've been running up the swear box pretty much full on this week.'

'Bad week for you, too?'

'Yeah, you know me. I really drown in everybody else's sorrows.'

'I couldn't do your job, but *you* are good at it.'

'Yeah, thanks, but we're straying here. Do you think he'll be here tonight – Simon, I mean? You going to say anything to the Bamras, or to him?'

'I was going to talk to Nasir or Amira, see if anyone's complained. I feel bad that I've only been here a few weeks and he's been here months, but still . . .'

'You *need* to, Jin. He's sexually harassing people and is getting away with it. I'll let Nick know, too.'

'You could ask Nick if anyone's reported Simon for it. He looked like he had something on Susie. She couldn't wait to get away, but I really wonder what would've happened if I hadn't intervened.'

'You think he'd have raped her?'

'I don't know, Ally. The guy's a chancer, I wouldn't put it past him.'

'Shit.' Both phones buzzed. 'Sorry, you're having to pay for my swearing for a change.'

'I'm sure I've run up your account plenty,' Jinny said as she turned up the long driveway. She parked behind the line of cars at the Towers. Charley was getting out of Ayesha's car in front of her. Jinny's heart skipped a beat. They'd met twice during the week for lunch and while Jinny was desperate to get to the next stage with Charley, she didn't want to frighten her off and end the relationship before it had a chance to blossom.

Inside the main room were groups of cushions, separated into different corners of the room. Ally rolled her eyes at Jinny. 'Great! What've you dragged me to tonight? Looks like we're in for some group work on the floor. I dread to think.'

'As long as I'm not in a group with Sleazy Simon, I'm okay with that.' Jinny scanned the room for him. 'Doesn't look like he's here. He's always in first, normally, but I suppose there's a first for everything.'

'Hope he isn't.' Ally shivered. 'Especially after what you've just told me. I saw him cornering you last week and trying to feel you up. Urgh.'

'Yeah, he showed me his bulging biceps from his gym workout then tried to feel mine. I told him if he touched me again I'd show him my fist in his face.'

'And yet he did. What a jerk. He deserves a fist in the face. I forgot to mention him to Nick before, but I certainly will now.'

'You know, if he *was* the rapist, he knew about the spell to protect the town. Maybe that's why it occurred outside town.'

'That's an interesting point. I promise I'll mention that to Nick, too.'

Amira and Nasir entered the room and beckoned everyone to take their seats on the usual circle of cushions. Amira did the relaxation meditation and then passed the session over to Nasir.

'I must say I was pleased to receive Jinny's email today, telling me about the kittens she's rescued.' Nasir nodded to her. 'And how pleased I am that there was the perfect number we require for familiars.'

'No, there wasn't,' whispered Ally. Jinny nudged

her.

'And to have the spell work so fast once again just helps solidify in my mind how gifted our coven is.'

Everyone was nodding and smiling in agreement at his words, except Ally who was crossing her eyes at Jinny. Jinny tried not to laugh and looked across at Charley who was smiling at her. Jinny had explained to Charley at one of their lunches how Ally's sceptic commentary throughout the meetings was tantamount to blasphemy. Charley vowed not to sit anywhere near Ally as she wouldn't be able to prevent herself from laughing hysterically. Although, she pleaded to hear all about it afterwards.

'However, I do want to take a few minutes of silence for the latest rape victim,' Nasir asked solemnly. 'While we asked for protection for the town, and got that, it just shows you how we need to be careful about what we ask for. Denise was from Covenston. So let's close our eyes for two minutes and send healing thoughts to Denise and her family.'

Nasir closed his eyes and bowed his head and everyone else followed suit. Jinny felt it was only reverent that she did the same. She sent out a wish for Denise to recover fast and strong. Then she had a peek at the others. Everyone still had their eyes closed and head bowed. Even Ally. Jinny closed hers again and thought of Charley. She wondered when or if Charley would confide more about her own rape. She wondered if all these current attacks made her feel scared or vulnerable. Maybe Jinny could ask her that.

'Thank you, everyone. I'm sure Denise will benefit from that. Now let's move on. Tonight, I want us to look at enhancing relationships.'

Jinny felt Ally nudge her again. 'If he suggests

we strip naked and get touchy feely, I'll be out the door before his pants hit the deck,' Ally whispered.

'Don't worry, I'll be hot on your tail.'

'. . . Get into groups where we want similar things. For example, Charley mentioned to me earlier, and she gave me permission to repeat this, that she would like a spell about finding a partner who loves her for who she is. And when I was speaking to Debbie,' Nasir nodded at Debbie, 'she asked for a spell that would enhance her relationship with a family member. So, if anyone wanting to work on a partner-type spell please head to the left of the room and anyone wanting to work on a family relationship spell go to the right of the room. Anyone want to work on any other type of spell?'

Everyone shook their heads. Jinny noticed Charley blushing but still brave enough to look her in the eye and raise an eyebrow. Jinny's heart nearly leaped into her throat. She couldn't help but beam back.

'Good, we seem to have that covered,' Nasir continued. 'I'll go to the family group and work with you. Amira will work with the partners' group. This time we want you to work together to develop your own spell.' Nasir stood up and went over to the left and Amira headed to the right.

Ally grabbed Jinny by the sleeve and headed towards Amira. 'I really could do with a shag,' she whispered.

'Maybe this spell will work for you and Nick then.'

'What do I have to lose?'

Jinny watched Charley head towards their group too. The four of them sat down, Jinny across from Amira, Charley and Ally on either side. Ally was smiling, or was she laughing inside? Jinny was unsure.

'Has anyone here tried their own spell?' Amira asked.

Ally's knee nudged at Jinny. Jinny wasn't going to admit her failed love spell so she gave Ally her 'keep schtum' look and said nothing.

'The important thing about spells is to make sure you ask for what you desire so specifically that the spell does not find a way to get you what you want with undesirable effects.'

Jinny felt her cheeks burn, but she still wouldn't admit her failings. Maybe one day, when she knew the coven better, she could have a laugh about it. The group worked for half an hour on a rhyming spell to bring them a love partner that would give them what they needed now, and into the future, for a lasting relationship. When they all agreed they were happy with their spell, Amira led them through its incantation. Jinny felt Charley squeeze her hand and looked up to catch her eye. There was no doubt Charley was flirting with her. She squeezed her hand back and Charley beamed at her, sending Jinny's heart fluttering. They'd already arranged to meet midweek, and Jinny didn't know how she would occupy herself till them. She was so distracted by Charley, she forgot to ask the Bamras about Simon. Next time, she silently promised herself on the drive home.

***

Ally

'Ally?' Sharon's voice cut through the stillness of my quiet office where I was reading up on some notes. 'Look who I found loitering outside.'

'Hmm?' I got up to see who Sharon was talking about. It was Charley.

'Hi. I was hoping you might have a few minutes for a quick chat?'

'Of course, Charley, come in.'

'God, I feel really awkward, like a kid.' She giggled nervously.

'Don't. We've known each other a while now. You know you can talk to me. What's up?' I closed the door as she flopped onto the sofa.

'I like Jinny,' she blurted out. 'I want to know you're okay with me seeing her.'

'I know you do, and she likes you – a lot. But you guys know I'm a like a mother hen wanting to protect you all. You've been through a great deal, and Jinny, well I'm worried that she's just finished a relationship and–'

'Ally, I know you're looking out for us, and for Jinny, and we've spoken about all that. I guess I came here, though, to tell you I'm ready. So's Jinny. We wanna go for it and we're adults. I just wanted you to know that it's not just Jinny, I feel the same way.'

'I'm glad you came here. I can't stop you or Jinny – I wouldn't. It's not up to me. You're right, you're both adults. Just go slow, yeah?'

'We will. I promise.' Charley beamed at me, looking relieved that she'd got her feelings off her chest and secured my clumsy approval. 'Look, I'm nipping to the café for a quick lunch now. You want to join me?'

Charley beamed some more. 'I'd love that. You don't mind me joining you?'

'Well, I wouldn't be asking if I did,' I teased her. She giggled again. 'Let's go.' I grabbed my bag and jacket and held the door open to let her go out in front of me.

'See you in an hour, Sharon,' I called, watching Charley ahead of me. I *was* happy for her; she deserved it.

***

Jinny felt the draught from the café door opening behind her as she worked from her laptop. She looked up to see Ally sitting down across from her and was delighted to see Charley slide into the seat beside her.

'This *is* a pleasant surprise,' she said to Charley.

'Hey, what about me?' Ally kicked her playfully under the table.

'I see you every day almost. No surprises there. Ow!' Ally kicked her again.

'I went to see Ally for an impromptu session.'

'Everything okay?' Jinny asked, immediately worried.

'Yes, more than,' Charley reassured her. 'Ally asked me to join you both for lunch. I hope that's okay?'

Jinny pulled her into a hug. Her two favourite people in the world; she couldn't be happier. Jinny waved Linda over. 'What do you want to eat, Charley? We'll have our usual, Linda.'

'Surprise me. Just get me what you're having.'

'Easy order,' Linda said retreating.

'Did you get a chance to tell Nick about Simon?' Jinny asked Ally.

'What about Simon?' Charley asked.

Jinny quickly explained about the gym incident.

'That's dreadful. And scary. You okay?' Charley put her hand on Jinny's leg and it felt good. Fi had avoided any contact with her in the latter months, so that simple touch was so powerful. She swallowed and hoped no one noticed her sentimental reaction.

Ally saved the moment and continued the conversation. 'I was going to let Nick know, but haven't had a chance. I'll pop into the station on my way back to the office. Actually, Charley, Jinny and I were wondering if he'd harassed anyone at the coven?'

'Oh God, yes he had.'

'Really?' Ally asked, looking at Jinny then back to Charley.

'Yeah, Debbie told me there was a girl there for a few months before Simon joined. It was before me. She said the girl, Leona, I think her name was, or Lindsay, something like that . . . Anyway, seems he followed her home one night and tried to get her to let him in. Luckily her neighbour in the flat above heard the commotion and told Simon she'd call the police if he didn't leave. The girl never came back to the coven. Debbie only found out weeks later when she met her shopping.'

'Jeez.' Jinny slapped her hand on the table. 'Did Debbie tell Amira or Nasir?'

'Yeah, but they said unless he did anything untoward to any of the coven members at the coven or outside it and they reported it, then they really couldn't do anything about it without direct evidence from the person themselves.'

'I see their point.' Ally nodded and sat back as Linda deposited their usual Thursday selections of lentil chilli and pitta pockets. 'Thanks, Linda. Smells fab – as normal.'

'Enjoy, everyone.'

'So he didn't act inappropriately to anyone else in the coven?' Jinny asked.

'Not as far as I'm aware,' Charley told them, filling her pitta with chilli.

'Apart from throwing some innuendoes at me and staring at my cleavage,' Jinny reminded everyone. 'I will say something to the Bamras next time I go – especially if he's there. I've no problem putting him in his place, but I get the impression he looks for people he thinks he can bully.'

'Yeah, you have to say something,' Ally agreed. 'He can't think he can get away with treating women like that, ever.'

Ally left after eating, leaving Charley to share some apple pie with Jinny, who asked, 'You fancy coming back to the flat . . . play with the kittens?'

'Yeah, you should've started with kittens! Lead the way. I'm not working till later today, so I've got a few hours.'

Jinny gathered up her belongings and nipped through the café to her place, Charley at her back. Charley went straight to the kittens, sat on the floor next to them and took a grey, sleeping one onto her lap.

'This one is my favourite. Can she be mine?'

'Yeah, Ally chose the black one.' Jinny sat down on the other side of the cat basket.

'So you're left with the black and white one?'

'Suits me. She's a little gem.'

'When does the mum go back to her owner?'

'Got a couple of weeks yet. She's on holiday now. Nirja, the vet nurse, says the longer they have to wean the better. More natural.'

Charley lifted the kitten to her face, took a deep breath and sighed. 'I love the smell of them. Don't you?'

Jinny laughed. 'I do. I sniff them too.' They laughed together.

Charley looked at Jinny and Jinny felt her heart kick up a beat. She hoped she was going to say she was ready for the next step, but Charley's face all of a sudden looked serious.

'I . . . I've never been with anyone since the rape, Jinny, but . . . Look, I want to be with you. I want to spend time with you, spend the night with you, see where it goes.' She rushed her speech. 'I'm just a little unsure . . .'

Jinny reached over and put an arm around her, pulling her shoulder to shoulder, head to head. 'Don't worry. I'm here for you. Just take it at your pace. I got you a spare key.'

'You did?'

'You don't need to take it.'

'I want to! Thank you.' Charley looked up at Jinny, tilting her chin up. She looked at Jinny's mouth and then into her eyes. Jinny answered the silent question with a tender touching of the lips. Charley's lips parted and her tongue tipped out to touch Jinny's, gently probing. Jinny deepened the kiss slowly, ready to pull back if Charley hesitated, but she didn't. Pausing, Charley put the kitten down and looked again at Jinny, her face flushed and smiling. 'Want to move to the sofa?'

'Hell, yeah.' Jinny smiled too, pulling Charley to her feet, and they kissed all the way to the sofa.

CHAPTER ELEVEN

Ally

Robyn Carruthers was waiting for me in the counselling room. She looked pale, thin and withdrawn as she took off her coat and sat down. As she unwound her woollen scarf, I noticed that her neck had residual yellow and purple bruising. The wounds and bruises on her body would heal eventually, but what about the emotional scars? She was so young, her life had barely begun.

'Robyn, did you come alone today?' I wanted to start somewhere easy.

'My father dropped me off. My mother's an emotional wreck. Maybe she should be here too?' Robyn sounded flat, emotionless. She would go through a grieving process, stages of denial, anger, depression, bargaining and, hopefully one day, acceptance. The process was different for everyone as they moved in and out, often repeating the process many times. It could take days, months or years. How would Robyn cope, I wondered?

'I want to take this at your pace. Can you tell me

152

about you? You go to college, don't you?'

'I was training to be a veterinary nurse. I guess I'm better around animals than people. It seemed like the best choice.'

'What about hobbies, activities. What do you like doing in your spare time?'

'I don't go out much. My parents have always been strict, over-protective. They never let me go anywhere with friends. I guess any friends I have ever had got fed up with me saying no to them.'

'Your mother said you used to help her at the care home and at the church.'

'Yeah. She encouraged me to do things like that. We'd go to the gym for a swim together. She'd say we were best buddies, but I knew it was her way of keeping an eye on me.' Her voice started to get louder as she opened up.

'You sound a little angry. Are you?' I pushed a little, trying to get in deeper.

'Yes,' she choked out. 'I had no life. And now . . . I'll have even less of one.' Tears streamed down her cheeks.

'It doesn't have to be that way. I know you might feel that everything has been taken away from you, but you can still have the life you wanted.'

'Really? I can't have kids – if I wanted that.'

'Did you?'

'I don't know, does it matter now?'

'At the hospital, you said you were a virgin. Have you ever had a boyfriend?'

'No. I'm gay. But my parents don't know. I've told no one, except the minister when I had counselling.'

'Counselling? I didn't know.'

'My mother wanted me to go for it, she said I was depressed. I was. You would be too, if you had no

153

life. Cooped up, frightened to live. It helped to talk to someone. It was good there. It was a group of four other women. All ages, all depressed. I felt safe there. Safe enough to come out. It was such a relief. Everyone was so supportive. I even jokingly called one of the women in the group, Ruth, mum. She was so maternal, like the mother I wanted. John even offered to help me broach the subject of my gayness with my parents. But there was no way they'd accept that – ever.'

Our counselling session progressed better than expected. Robyn was more talkative than I'd anticipated, her anger driving her. I wondered if that was because she'd led an isolated, friendless life. I was sad for her. A child tied to their mother's apron strings often grew up timid, frightened to branch out into the world. Would this tragedy make that inevitable for Robyn? Her childhood was such a stark contrast to my own. Jinny and I grew up with supportive parents that encouraged us to be happy and free. We had boundaries to keep us safe, but we were encouraged to explore and be inquisitive and we were friends as well as sisters. Our parents always reminded us to be there for each other as we grew up. I was grateful for my childhood experiences, but I sometimes wondered if my blissful naivety had left me vulnerable to the sadness I so often endured when I felt overwhelmed as an adult.

I looked at my notebook. Several things stood out to me and I had underlined them during the session. Robyn had mentioned the going to the gym; she was a member, like Gill. What about Denise? I wasn't sure if the police had checked that. Was this what linked the women? I thought briefly about what Jinny had said about Simon. I didn't want to go around pointing the finger at every would-be

Casanova, but it wouldn't hurt to get Nick or Jake to look at his background.

I also pondered the fact that Robyn said she was gay. Denise was gay. But Gill wasn't. Jeez, was I jumping to all sorts of ridiculous conclusions? After all, no one knew that Robyn was gay, except for the minister and the counselling group. I asked Robyn for permission to speak with John, maybe he could shed some more light on why someone would make a victim out of this quiet, lonely girl.

***

The officer at the desk said Nick was in a meeting, but Jake would come and speak to me. She pointed me towards their empty office, which I was already familiar with. As I walked to the office I could see Nick in the conference room at the end of the corridor. The door was shut and I couldn't hear what he was saying, but his gesturing looked frustrated. I was just about to turn into the office when the person he was talking to stood up, walked around the table and into his arms. I stood transfixed as his arms went around her.

'Hey, Ally. What brings you in?' I jumped at Jake's voice as he opened the door. He noticed where I was looking and guided me in, closing the door behind me. 'Nick's dealing with some personal stuff, so you've got me. What can I do for you?'

I was so distracted by what I'd seen, I had to rack my brain to focus on why I was there.

'I . . . I wanted to talk to Ni . . . you about a couple of things.' I wished I'd brought my notebook of the issues as my mind was blank. Well, not blank; the image of Nick with his arms wrapped around a woman was etched in silhouette when I closed my eyes. I took a deep breath and said I had a few things to discuss. Jake lifted a notebook from his desk, opened it where his pen was and wrote in the date without saying anything.

'I saw Robyn today,' I added. He stopped writing and looked up as he waited to hear what I had to say. 'She said a couple of things that I thought may be important. First, that she was a member of the gym, same as Gill. I wondered if Denise was also? Secondly, and this is in confidence . . .' He nodded. 'She told me she was gay. She gave me permission to let you know, but asked that it go no further. Her parents don't know, and she doesn't want them to.' Jake scribbled down what I'd said – or maybe he was writing that I was a nuisance, looking for any excuse to come and see Nick.

'So she's only told you she's gay?'

'No. She was getting counselling for depression in one of the minister's self-help groups. She told them. So you might want to look into that.' I paused when I saw his eyebrows go up and the muscle in his jaw twitch. Obviously he didn't like being told how to do his job. I shut up and shrugged my shoulders. Was I coming across as some ridiculous, amateur detective? Maybe he knew all this already. I could feel my cheeks redden. I felt relieved that I'd said something though. I watched Jake as he wrote more notes, hoping that Nick might appear through the door, but he didn't.

'Okay, that could be important. We are looking at the gym, and people that were there that night. We're about half way through checking all the staff and members. Nothing sticks out so far,' Jake answered. 'Denise *was* a member so, yes, it's our first real connection between the victims. But hell, it's the only gym in the town – I'm a member myself – so it

156

might be just coincidence.'

'There's something else. Er . . .' I hesitated again because I knew I was running the risk of getting bodily escorted out of the police station. But I'd promised Jinny.

'There's a guy at a cov . . . club my sister and I are in. There's something off about him.'

'Ally, please tell me you've got more than a vague feeling about some creep in a club?' Jake rolled his eyes and stood up. He was close to losing it.

'There is, Jake. I know how it sounds, but I've worked with people for years and I've got a gut feeling about this guy. He's a bully. Jinny caught him harassing a woman outside of the gym, which he's also a member of . . . and he was there on the night Gill was raped. His name's Simon Hargreaves. He's a touchy-feely creep that likes to overstep his boundaries and doesn't like hearing the word no. Please, just check him out.' I sounded desperate.

Jake stood up; I guessed that was it. I was trying to think if I had anything else to tell him, but my mind kept going back to Nick. As I left the office, Jake followed me out. I tried to see past him into the conference room but Jake stepped to the side, blocking my line of sight.

'Hargreaves will be checked along with the rest of the members. Let me know if any of your other patients say anything or remember anything more that could be useful. And Ally, leave the police work to us.'

Let *him* know, not Nick. Great. Leave the police work to *them*. I felt like a kid being told off. Now I'd never find out who the woman was. Why the hell did Nick lead me on? Or did he? Christ, I felt such a fool as I banged the car door shut. I didn't know whether to scream in anger or cry. But Nick Daniels wasn't going to stop me doing my bit to protect innocent women.

The church felt eerily cold and damp as I entered. I wasn't a churchgoer; organised religion just seemed like a good way to keep good people divided and more easily controlled. Being more of a spiritual person, I wanted to believe that people were inherently good and although I was not religious, I still wanted to believe that there was a greater force looking out for us.

'Ally?' John looked up, from his task of placing pamphlets at the end of each pew, to greet me with a warm, yet questioning welcome.

'Hi, John. I tried to call but there was no answer at the rectory.'

'No, I've been here putting out the new hymn sheets. How can I help you? Are you okay? You look tired, Ally.'

'I'm fine. Just a little frazzled that the cops are no further forward with the investigation, that's all. I spoke with Robyn Carruthers today. She said you'd counselled her.'

'Ah Robyn. How is she? I was worried, she's so young. It's terrible what has happened to her, and to the other women.' He shook his head.

I wondered if he, as I did, felt the weight of all his counselling clients pressing down on him. Or maybe his God helped him to feel supported.

'Hopefully with our help she can recover,' I offered. 'She told me she was gay, but she hadn't broached the subject with her parents . . . or with anyone, in fact. She's quite a loner.'

'Yes, her parents are . . . er . . . quite protective. Her mother, in particular, is taking the rape quite badly. I spoke to her about this at the hospital, said she wouldn't be able to help Robyn recover if she was a wreck herself and so reluctantly she agreed to call

158

Anne for an appointment.'

'Anne? I'm sorry – who?'

'Anne. Anne Bishopton. She works a few days a week here at the church. She keeps my appointments for me. Voluntarily, of course, I can't afford to pay for a secretary and as she's an active church member, it makes sense to have someone that I know and trust to help with my various duties.'

'I didn't know this. When me, Sharon, or any of our counsellors refer clients, it's only ever been yourself we've spoken to.'

'Ah, that's because Anne has only recently increased her duties. She wanted to do more. Probably to get her away from Bill more, especially after his last misdemeanour. She's very forgiving. She said helping me more was better for her and I gladly accepted her offer,' he explained while he carried on placing the hymn sheets out. I followed him as he moved.

'So it's not just the counselling group that knew Robyn was gay; Anne had access to that information too?' I didn't like hearing myself make the accusation but this case was becoming more complicated with every passing day.

'Why would that be a problem, Ally? Anne has worked for me for several years. She has transcribed my dictated notes, kept my files orderly and now keeps my appointments. I think she understands client confidentiality more than most, especially given her own ... er ... situation.'

'I get it, John, I'm sure you're right. But couples talk, conversation over dinner and the likes. We don't know how much Bill knows about Robyn, and he was questioned on his homophobic abuse.'

'I'm sure Anne doesn't talk much to Bill about these sorts of things. I wouldn't want her to get into

159

trouble.'

'I'm sure you're right. I'm surprised she didn't come to you for counselling, then, given her Church connections. Especially as I referred her to the refuge.'

'I tried to talk to her many times about Bill. He's not very good at ensuring Anne's beatings are not visible. She's always refused help. And anyway, it was her sister was it not, that got her to see you? Debbie isn't much of a churchgoer.'

'Thanks for confirming that. Er . . . I forgot I have an appointment that I need to get to, so . . .' It sounded like an excuse because it was; I was rubbish at lying. This was now something else I was going to have to raise with Jake or Nick. Luckily, I'd see one of them at the self-defence class later.

***

Was it the posters decorating every lamppost, or the outright fear stalking the town that ensured the community hall was buzzing with women of all ages, ready to take part in the first self-defence class? Ally wasn't sure, she was just happy to see such a large turnout. She wandered round the room, chatting briefly to small groups of women. There was an aura of trepidation mingled with excitement, she thought, as she caught snatches of conversation about the rapes and the investigation. As she came to a stop next to Jinny and Charley – standing closely together, mesmerized by each other, already looking like a couple – the community hall door swung open and in walked Jake De Stefano with another guy. Jake smiled and motioned to Ally to join them. Jinny nudged her encouragingly to the front of the hall.

'Ally, this is Ken Chalmers – the instructor that

Nick recommended. Could you thank everyone for coming and introduce him to the class? I think it'd be a good way to start, seeing as most of the community know you.'

Ken nodded in agreement and shook Ally's hand firmly. He was medium height with fair hair. It was obvious he was fit, from his thin, wiry and well-toned physique. 'Don't worry, just do a quick hello, introduce me and I'll explain a bit about myself and the class,' he said smiling warmly.

'Okay.' Ally stepped forward to the front of the stage. 'Welcome everyone.' She paused, waiting for the crowd to settle, while a few women, including Jinny, voiced some 'shhhs' to the room. 'Thanks for coming out on this cold, dark, wet night but I do think you will all enjoy the evening. Some housekeeping first. Refreshments will be available in the kitchen during the break and if you hear the fire alarm the exits are through the kitchen, or to the side here and the main entrance. Okay, the two gentleman here are Detective Inspector Jake De Stefano and Ken Chalmers. Jake is one of the detectives involved with the ongoing investigation and Ken will be our instructor tonight, so let's give him a warm welcome.'

Ken smiled at everyone's applause as he took to the floor and briefly introduced himself, explaining his training background and what to expect in the first lesson. After a quick warm up, he asked the women to get into pairs; each woman would get a chance to be victim and perpetrator. Jinny and Charley linked arms, declaring themselves a pair, as Ally looked for any stray woman, like herself, needing a partner.

'Ally, you can pair with me because Ken is going to need us to do the demos,' Jake said, grabbing Ally's arm to keep her to the front of the hall.

'Oh gawd.' Ally cringed. She hated being put on the spot and she could've murdered Jinny and Charley, who were currently giggling like teenagers at her predicament.

'Don't worry, you're in good hands.' Ally could feel Jake's warm breath against her ear as he leaned closer.

Why couldn't this have been Nick?

Ally felt slightly embarrassed and a little amused knowing that Jake was toying with her.

'You don't like me, do you, Jake? Why?' Ally surprised herself at her own honesty and wondered if she'd get an equally honest reply.

Jake stepped in close and dropped her to the floor, as instructed by Ken. 'It's not you, Ally,' he replied as she got back up on her feet to practice the move again. 'You remind me of my ex. She was a counsellor, too. Broke my heart. It's hard to forgive. You look like the sort of woman who's broken plenty of hearts. Are you?' He looked her in the eye questioningly and Ally understood the reason for his initial coolness. He was still hurting.

The lesson progressed well with Ken showing the women how to use their voices and bodies against potential attackers. Under his instruction, Jake and Ally demonstrated various punching and striking movements, while Ken moved through the groups, fixing postures and clarifying the techniques. Ally realised that despite her initial reservations, she was enjoying herself, and Jake was a good partner. Entwined with him after one, poorly performed technique, they were laughing loudly together before he reached down and pulled her upright. As they fell into each other's arms comfortably Ally looked up over Jake's shoulder to see Nick watching bemusedly from the doorway. Her cheeks reddened.

162

Shit. How long has he been watching for?

She knew their action could be interpreted as flirting, and maybe it was. Ally nodded to Nick and tried to focus more on what Ken was saying as he started to bring the class to a conclusion. While he took some final questions Nick approached Jake and Ally.

'You guys were looking good up there,' Nick said to them both while looking directly at Ally.

Well this is awkward.

Ally pulled on her hoodie to ease her embarrassment. 'Yeah, Ken is a great instructor. Thanks for setting this up, everyone really enjoyed it. Most have said they're already looking forward to next week.'

'You missed a good training opportunity, Nick,' Jake added. 'We were talking earlier about breaking hearts but, I think from that session, Ally's pretty good at breaking balls too, eh?' Jake laughed.

'Erm . . . Could I talk to you guys about something?' Ally asked quickly, making use of the upbeat moment before she lost her nerve.

'I need to get back to the office, Nick. I've got to finish some paperwork before I head off for the night.' Jake excused himself, leaving Ally standing with Nick.

'Yep, see you tomorrow.' Nick patted him on the shoulder and turned to Ally. 'Looks like the cleaners are wanting to get in, shall we head out?'

'Ally.' Jinny caught her arm. 'Oh, hi Nick. Charley and I are heading back to mine. D'you want us to drop you off at home? I can't see your car in the carpark.'

'That's because I left it at work,' Ally admitted. 'I was just going to ride back with you guys and run into work tomorrow.'

163

'It's okay, Jinny. I've got her. I'll make sure she gets home okay,' Nick answered for Ally. 'Is that alright?'

'Ah, yeah, th . . . that's great, thanks Nick. Looks like I'm sorted, Jinny. Speak later.'

'You are that,' Jinny replied sarcastically, winking at Ally.

'I'm not far, do you want to come back for a coffee?' Ally crossed her fingers inside her jacket.

'That's fine, I was heading home for the evening anyway.'

***

Ally

He's gorgeous.

I admired his profile as he drove. I loved the way he pushed his hand through that sexy hair all the time. And finally, here he was with me, just me. We fell into an easy chat about our tastes in music and film. This was the side of him I didn't know, the relaxed, sociable Nick. He smiled as he chatted, his eyes twinkling. Here I was thinking how gorgeous he was when I caught sight of myself in the car outside mirror. Jeez, my hair looked like a thatched roof after a storm – what must he be thinking? I smoothed my hair as we arrived at my home, a detached cottage in a quiet, leafy, residential street. It felt semi-rural but it was only a few minutes drive from the town centre. The cottage had two bedrooms, a real fireplace and had been fully renovated to look clean and contemporary on the inside with a large, open plan kitchen and dining area. I was glad that the previous owners had kept the lounge as a separate room. I loved to snuggle up every night on the sofa, watching telly in front of the fire.

'Come in, please. Just go into the lounge and I'll get us a coffee.' I pushed open the door, motioning for him to go in. I was picking up stray shoes and discarded items along the way, a pathetic attempt at tidying up but hopefully he wasn't the sort to notice.

'Can I help?' Nick startled me as I was shakily spooning coffee into the filter pot. Could he see how nervous I was? He put his hand over mine, taking the spoon from me, and continued making the coffee. 'You got any biscuits? I'm starving.' He grinned. 'You have a nice place here. Been here long?'

'A few years now. I fell in love with it the first time I viewed it and luckily I had some savings and an old trust fund which helped me to buy it,' I replied, rummaging for some biscuits.

'So, what did you want to chat about?' he asked, after some general chit chat about the property market.

I sighed, not wanting to break the easy momentum we had. It felt good getting to know him. 'Did Jake tell you I had called in to tell you about Robyn Carruthers?'

'Yes, you said she was gay. Like Denise. It could be a connection, a homophobic attack. I've got officers looking at various leads, including that. Gill Garby doesn't fit into that equation, but we'll look anyway.'

'I found out something else. Anne Bishopton keeps the minister's appointment book for his counselling sessions. Counselling sessions where Robyn admitted she was gay.'

'Ally, Bill Bishopton has an alibi for all those rapes.'

'Who? Anne? A woman he beat regularly into submission? And who could be feeding him vital

165

information, knowingly or unknowingly. Come on, Nick, surely you didn't just take him at his word?'

'We didn't just *do* anything, Ally. We can't keep people in the cells hoping they'll give in and admit to things that they did or didn't do with no solid evidence. We've been through this already.' He slammed his mug down.

'I also told Jake about Simon Hargreaves when I came to see *you* yesterday,'

'Jake said. He also said that you had to leave the police work to us.'

'Really? You were the one that wanted my help. I thought that's what I was doing.' Our voices were raised. This wasn't the romantic interlude I'd hoped for, more like world war three.

'I asked you to help with the victims' counselling, Ally, not investigating.'

'Well, maybe if you had someone behind bars, Nick, I wouldn't feel the need to investigate.' That was too much. I had overstepped the mark.

Subtle Ally, very subtle.

'We may not be doing a good enough job for you, Ally, but CID are more than happy with the investigation. We're following all regular protocols and Gill's reconstruction will air on Wednesday, which should bring in more leads, as well.'

'You did the reconstruction already? No one said.' I couldn't believe it, I was being shut out – or so it felt.

'I didn't realise we needed to call you for permission before we made any moves.' He stood up, looking furious. 'I'd better go. Thanks for the coffee – and the criticism.'

I followed him to the door knowing I'd blown it. 'Nick, I–'

'Save it, Ally.'

166

The walls shook as he banged the door on his way out. I stood behind it, the noise echoing in my ears, as I slammed my fists off the wood. Then I heard him say my name from the other side of the door. I took a breath and opened it. His eyes were dark, serious and wanting. Or maybe that was me. I wasn't sure who reached out first but we latched on to each other, kissing hungrily as he pushed me back into the hall, kicking the door shut. His lips crushed mine as he reached under my hoodie for my breast, feeling my nipple harden under his touch. A moan escaped my throat and he quickly helped me out of the top. My fingers combed through his hair as his mouth bent to my breast, sucking gently on my already hardened nipple. God, how I'd longed for this. An image of the woman I'd seen him embracing yesterday came rudely to my thoughts and I faltered.

'Nick, I–'

'Shhh,' he said, his lips finding mine again. So I let it go, giving in to the heat that was surging between us. We kissed and undressed, dropping our clothes as we stumbled to my bedroom and fell onto the bed, me on top. I felt my urge rising and his hardness against my stomach so I stroked his length, watching his eyes lock with mine, enjoying the sheer, unchecked, sexual pleasure. He stopped briefly to rip the corner of a condom packet with his teeth, then slipped it on with ease. With the protection in place, I guided him into me, liking the way he groaned huskily against my ear as he slid deeper inside me. Moving together, fast then slow, enjoying the pace, his fingers coaxed me to climax, then he too let go, both of us relishing the last pulses of our orgasm. The whole thing was over faster than either of us intended. Had he felt as I did? I allowed myself to believe he had, until another thought of the mysterious woman crept into my mind. I'd have to find out who she was, especially as I had strict personal rules on cheating. I didn't ever want to be the reason someone's relationship ended, and I certainly didn't want anyone doing likewise to me. I'd ask him, just not in our post sex glow.

Our legs still tangled we kissed slowly until Nick's mobile vibrated in his jeans, which lay crumpled on the floor.

'Sorry, I'd better get that.' He got up and my eyes took in his toned, slender body, wondering how often he exercised to keep that six-pack in shape. 'Jake? Yeah, go on. Right. okay. Yeah, I'll tell Ally. See you tomorrow. Thanks.'

'Is everything okay?' I asked, watching as he looked around for his boxer shorts.

'Hargreaves has priors, Jake's bringing him in. I need to go. This doesn't mean you're off the hook, Ally. You need to take a step back now, it's too dangerous.'

I was surprised at his intimation. I hadn't thought that I may be putting myself at risk playing amateur Sherlock Holmes. He was right. I just wasn't sure I could leave it though. I cared too much.

***

Jinny

As the glow from the cabernet sauvignon warmed me, I smiled at Charley who was sitting across the table from me, still spooning her pink sorbet. Her lush pink lips were swollen with the icy dessert and I wondered if they'd taste of raspberry. We'd both taken turns in the shower when we got back from self-defence. I went first so I could prepare dinner when Charley was in. And now she sat there teasing me by wearing nothing but one of my long T-shirts – and she knew it. She licked her lips and grabbed my hand.

'Come, sit over where it's comfy. I want to talk.'

Leaving my wine on the table, I let her drag me over to the sofa. We both knew what was coming. I was nervous, probably more than she was. I was afraid I might not react the way she'd want me to or expect me to, but how did you react when the person you love is going to tell you about something that hurt her badly?

I sat in the corner of the three-seater, and Charley sat at the far end of it to face me. Was she afraid of close contact as she laid herself bare? I just wanted to hold her and tell her it was okay, I didn't need to know. But I kept quiet and kept my distance, because it's how Charley wanted it. And she needed to tell me.

'There's not much I can tell you about the rape, Jinny, I still don't remember it. Maybe that's for the best. Ally said it would come back when my mind felt I was ready to deal with it. All I remember is from what people said and I don't know how much of that is my memory or theirs.' She laughed nervously as she thought back. 'I was a first-year nursing student at the time. I came home to help mum with dad, who'd had a stroke. I hated the bastard, and I don't feel bad for saying so. He was crazy with power and treated mum like shite, but she let him. Part of her liked the importance of being a judge's wife, she liked wielding his authority and so she let him bully her into conforming to his rules. I was so glad to get away.'

I just nodded and let her talk. I didn't know her

family well. They'd lived at the opposite end of town and had gone to the Catholic school. I always wondered why John became a minister and not a priest; a question for another time, I thought.

'Poor John stayed on to help mum, taking on local jobs, but he'd always intended to go to university. So when I got back, it relieved the pressure on him and he went off to some university open days, while I helped out. I'd told John I was gay, and to be honest, I think that's why he'd left. I'm sure he didn't want to face the music when I told mum. He knew she wouldn't like it. She didn't, and neither did Dad.' She looked at me and took a deep breath. 'In fact, my news killed them both.'

'No–' I tried to reassure her that that was unlikely, but she raised her hand to stop me, shaking her head as she explained what happened - how she'd tried to kill herself, John helping her through that, and then coming back to Covenston. I could see she just wanted to set the scene and get it all out in the open between us. I'd already told her about Fiona, and my realisation that I didn't actually love her anymore. And that I felt about Charley in a way I thought I'd never feel again after Beth. I brought my attention back to her as she was telling me about feeling safe back home. Until the rapes.

'All I remember was coming to as paramedics were tending to me. I'd been beaten to a pulp as well as raped. I had concussion; there wasn't a part of my body that wasn't bruised or bloody, inside and out. It took weeks for the internal bruising to go down. He'd used a brush handle to try damage me. I had a catheter in for weeks till the swelling went down and I could pee properly again.' Charley stopped briefly to check I wasn't horrified by her revelations. 'I was in hospital for a long time. It took me an even longer time before I could consider a sexual relationship, or even touch myself . . . and not till I saw you before I could . . . well, you know?

I watched her cheeks redden, but I was glad that she'd been fantasising about me just as much as I was about her. My heart raced. I wanted to hold her in my arms, but she wasn't finished. I nodded, though.

She smiled. 'And now I want to do more than just touch myself, Jinny.' She slid across the sofa to me and touched my hair. I had a lump in my throat at the vulnerability in her eyes. My hand cupped her cheek and wiped away the single tear that dropped from her eye. She put her lips on mine, gently at first then more demanding. I was lost to her. We kissed and tentatively I touched her breast, afraid she'd pull away. Instead, she pushed closer and her hands sought my breasts under my T-shirt. Her touch on my bare skin brought a heat and swelling down below that made me ache for her touch. She pulled away from me, her eyes glazed and she beamed at me as she pulled her top off. She was naked below it, her nipples pert and dark pink and her pubic triangle, blonde. There was nothing artificial about Charley, inside and out.

I pulled off my T-shirt and my pants as she gazed over me, still smiling. She moved over me as I lay beneath her and I felt weak with desire as she gently lay her body on top of mine. She moaned in pleasure as I ran my hands down her back and over her lovely muscly backside. She pressed her pubic bone against mine as I nuzzled into her neck, smelling the sweet vanilla in her hair. Her mouth found my breast and I gasped in pleasure as she sucked each one in turn. I turned around so we were both lying on our sides. I kissed her hard on the mouth and slowly trailed kisses to her nipple. It was so delicate and peaked to firmness as I sucked. One hand cupped her other breast, so firm and small, enough to fill my hand. My other hand moved slowly and gently down between us. She smiled at me as she lifted her top leg and wrapped it about my hip. I kept watching her as I gently slipped over her swollen clitoris and slid inside her moistness. Her eyes closed and her head went back as she moaned in pleasure. With my thumb on her clitoris, I felt her climax clench tightly as it pulsed around my fingers.

'Oh, fuck me, I've waited years for that, Jinny.' Charley laughed and cried at the same time. 'And now it's my turn,' she said as her hand slid down my body and her fingers entered my wetness. 'Now I'm going to make you scream with pleasure . . .'

And she did.

***

Jinny and Charley couldn't sit close enough at breakfast, sharing freshly-made oat pancakes, dripping in maple syrup and topped with crispy bacon flavoured seitan. Even Linda and Roz couldn't keep their smiles off their faces as they served them.

'You know I was thinking,' Charley said with a flirtatious look, 'that we could use some toys, next time . . .'

'Charley Proctor, you positively shock me.'

'I just want to start rewriting my history. Last night was so wonderful.'

'Well, if it's toys you want, I have a lovely collection I've never used. I bought them after Fiona, but hadn't even thought about them till now. I just needed to think of you to come . . .'

Charley laughed and shushed her. 'Good. That's just perfect then. I can't wait.' She giggled and nudged

Jinny under the table.

'You two were obviously up to no good.' Ally loomed over them, her entrance completely unnoticed. 'Stop the touchy-feely under the table, please. I want to see all hands on deck. Come on . . .' Ally slid into the seat opposite. Inside she was happy to see Jinny and Charley so engrossed. They both deserved a shot at love.

'What's up with your face, sis? Bit grumpy this morning. Not sleep well?'

'Not really.'

'Well? Elaborate . . .' Jinny prodded, and Charley nodded.

Ally reddened. 'It's not just you two who can have a . . . a bit of . . . you know?'

'You did it! At last. So how was detective Nickerless?' Jinny joked. Charley looked shocked. 'She's been hankering after him for a while,' she explained to Charley. 'And how come your face is so glum, Ally, when you got your lady garden watered at long last?'

'Oh my God, lady garden. That's beautiful,' approved Charley.

'Please, you two. You're acting like teenagers. He came . . .' Charley and Jinny laughed hysterically. Ally struggled to keep a straight face, waiting till the hilarity subsided before continuing, '. . . he saw, he conquered, and then buggered off to work.' Her phoned vibrated in her pocket. She took it out and put it on the table.

Jinny and Charley sobered.

'In the middle of the night?' Charley asked.

'Oh no. Well before night could begin. I didn't even get a chance to ask about . . .' Ally broke off. She hadn't said anything to Jinny about the other woman, and she felt guilty at having shagged Nick before getting to the bottom of that. Had she just fucked up a relationship she knew nothing about? Really though, if he was that quick to shag someone else, he had no morals and that wasn't the kind of person she wanted to get involved with. What a mess. Why had she been so impetuous?

Ally realised Jinny and Charley were staring at her. Had they said something?

'Ask him about what?' Jinny prompted.

'Oh, er . . . about Simon. I'd told him about Simon and I'd wanted to ask him more about it when he got a call.' She leaned in to whisper. 'Now this goes nowhere, okay?' Jinny and Charley nodded, leaning in, too. 'They'd brought Simon in for questioning. He's had priors.'

'Priors in what?' Jinny asked a little louder than Ally preferred.

'Shhh. I don't know. That's all Nick said before he left. When I know more I'll let you know.' Ally didn't mention any more about Anne Bishopton either. She felt it wasn't professional, and discussing rapes or the victims in Charley's presence would be inappropriate. Best to speak to Jinny alone, if she was ever going to get her alone . . . Ally watched as Jinny placed the last bit of pancake on the fork and fed it to Charley. She tried her best not to roll her eyes and was grateful when Linda put her coffee in front of her. Linda nodded at the two enthralled lovers and rolled her own eyes upwards. Ally nodded and rolled hers back.

'You finished with that plate, Jinny?' Linda was already lifting it and walking away.

'Jeez, the service in here . . .' Jinny called after her.

Linda turned and stuck out her tongue.

They all laughed.

'So that's good, they're questioning Mr Sleaze

himself. Did you tell him–'

'Yep, I told them everything you witnessed. At first I thought they were going to ignore it, because it was Jake I told and he asked me to butt out.'

'I thought they'd asked for your help?'

'They had. I reminded them of that.'

'Will he let you know about Simon?'

'I think so. Probably.' Ally wasn't so sure now. She wasn't sure about anything really. She didn't even know when she'd see him again.

'So, the spell worked,' Jinny announced.

'Hmm?' Ally wondered if Jinny and Charley had been doing spells on their own.

'The relationship spell,' Charley agreed nodding her head in delight. 'It did! The three of us certainly got a sh–' Jinny cupped a hand over Charley's mouth as they both laughed.

'You two are just unbearable today.'

'Come on, Ally,' Jinny chided. 'Can't you see it worked? Why won't you admit it? Spells work.'

'It's just coincidence.'

'How can you say that?'

'I told you. Everything is easily explained. I've been after Nick since well before the spell and you two . . . Well, you two've been ogling each other since you met. So saying it's the spell just doesn't cut it with me.'

'But really, Ally? You hadn't even made any moves on Nick and then – bam! It happens. That's not coincidence,' Jinny argued.

'I can see both your viewpoints,' Charley admitted. 'But to be honest I'm favouring the spells, based on repeatability.'

'I'm not convinced.' Ally shook her head, but she had doubts. She had wanted Nick, but she had also wanted to make sure he wasn't in a relationship before she jumped his bones. And it annoyed her that she had acted so irrationally. It would be nice to be able to blame something outside her control, but that wasn't her style. She had the hots for Nick and it got in the way of her normally rational behaviour. It was that simple. Ally's phone rang just as Jinny was about to launch into counter argument. Saved by the bell. 'Ally Canessa?'

'It's me. Nick.'

Ally laughed quietly. No mistaking that sexy voice. 'Hi Nick, what's up?'

'We had to let Simon Hargreaves go.'

'Why? So soon? I though you said he had priors.'

'He did. Two. Sexual assault. Had even tried to choke one girl before she got away.'

'God, Nick. Do you think he's the rapist?'

'He's got an alibi for every rape. And his charges were dropped. They were in different towns and according to him, they were misunderstandings, and no further action was taken.'

'What happened? Can you tell me more?'

'Later. Need to go.'

'Nick, who alibied him here?'

'His parents did.'

'And elsewhere?'

'Yes, Ally. His parents there too. And his father was the mayor in Simon's old hometown.'

'And you're not a bit suspect?'

'Ally, I told you. Keep out of it. Let us do our job. We know what we're doing.'

'But Nick–'

'And keep away from Simon Hargreaves. Tell your sister to do the same.'

'I will.' Ally was grateful for his concern, but she still had to talk to him, see where they stood. 'Er . . .

176

what about that other thing we discussed?' Ally was aware Jinny and Charley were listening and looking at each other, then back at Ally. She couldn't talk properly to Nick here.

'What? The Bishoptons?'

'Yes.' Ally was relieved he remembered.

'As I said, we're looking into all angles, Ally. Please, keep out of it now. Okay?'

'Okaaay,' she capitulated.

'Speak later.' He ended the call.

Ally was left staring at Jinny and Charley. 'Bye, then. See you later,' she told her silent phone and smiled at her audience.

'So, from your reaction, we take it they let Simon go?' Jinny asked.

'They had to. He had an alibi, but I think they're still keeping him on their radar from what Nick intimated. I'm still not going to the coven if he's still there, though.'

'Actually, I don't think he's getting back in,' Charley told them. 'Debbie said the coven weren't happy about how he was behaving and they complained to the Bamras. So Nasir told him he'd been expelled from the group for acting inappropriately. Word is Simon threatened them, said he'd cast his own spell and make every one of the coven members pay.'

'Bloody hell!' Ally's phone vibrated at Jinny's expletive.

'That's brilliant,' Charley said referring to the swear box app. Then, 'Nasir told him that his threat would be reported to the police. Debbie said he'd hung up before he heard the warning.'

'Did Nasir tell the police?' Ally asked.

'I don't know,' Charley admitted. 'Debbie never said. I'll ask her later today.'

177

'If she says he didn't, could you ask her to advise them to do so?'

'Of course. Leave it with me.' Charley stood and grabbed her bag from under the chair. Her kiss lingered on Jinny's lips, then, much to Ally's surprise, she bent in and kissed Ally on the cheek. 'Ciao, you two. Later?' she asked Jinny.

'Later.' Jinny beamed back.

'It's great to see her happy. I had my doubts about you and her, but I can see I had no need to worry.'

'Ally, I know it's early, but she's the one.' Jinny's eyes sparkled.

Ally patted her hand. 'I think you're right. Charley's a different person. Better. Healed. You did that.'

'Nah, you got her there. She was ready to be herself. And what about you? When are you seeing Nick again?'

'He said later. I presume he means today. Look, I'd better get to work. Nick says to keep away from Simon. And after what Charley's just told us, I'd be happier if you didn't go to the gym either.'

'Ally, I can't curtail my activities because Simon's a fucking bully.'

Ally put her phone in her bag after Jinny's profanity and gave her an annoyed look. It was always Ally's swear box that took the battering when Jinny was around. She was getting wise to that. 'I'm just worried.'

'Ally, I can handle Simon. Don't worry about me. I'll text you if and when I go and when I'm back. Okay?'

'Yeah, okay.' Ally drained her coffee, grabbed her bag and left. It was going to be a long day, she thought, hoping she'd see Nick at some point. Or maybe she'd drop in to see him after work if she didn't hear from him before then. Then she changed her mind. She refused to chase him – yet.

CHAPTER TWELVE

You lie here, waiting, among the floral scents and numerous shoes all paired neatly on racks, the rays of setting sunlight bleeding through the cracks in the cupboard door. They're just like your childhood memories seeping their way into your thoughts. Memories once pushed far away, hidden from everyday thoughts, just like the old picture scrapbooks tucked away at the back of this cupboard. You can see your younger self cowering in the corner, tear stains engrained in your dirty schoolboy face. You didn't understand then why your father shouted those words. His face red, his bloodshot eyes open and wide as he beat you with his belt. You were evil spawn. You deserved his punishment. Mother said you were brought to them so that they could undo the damage and guide you. Their love is working through you in the fixes you perform.

You look through the old photographs as you wait. College students, drunk and laughing at their cheap, immoral lives. There's nothing here to make you question your actions, they deserve your help just as you deserved your parents' help. What goes around, comes around.

You hear tyres on the gravel outside. She's home. Good, your legs are cramping inside here. Sounds of her talking on her mobile get louder as she comes upstairs.

'Yeah, I'm just real tired . . . uh-huh . . . it's to be expected at this stage. I'm going to lie down for a bit. In fact, I think I'll just stay in bed all evening, catch up on some zeds. Oh – my phone's about to die. I'll see you tomorrow morn– actually no, it'll be the afternoon, I've got that appointment in the morning. Okay. Love you too.'

Listen to the cunt blowing kisses down the phone. It makes you angry. It confirms your duty to the intervention. You need to focus now. This was a good place to wait. You instinctively knew she'd come here first. Through the crack in the door you can see her throw the mobile onto the bed and kick off her stilettos. Shoes that sluts wear. Her feet look swollen as she unbuttons her shirt, unzips her skirt and drops it around her ankles. This is it. The bitch is making it too easy for you. Sliding the cupboard door aside you stand behind her. Without the heels you see that she's small, an easy prey. As the hood goes on and you pull the cord tight, tighter, she flails about, choking, trying to grab stuff off her dresser. You love this part as they become unconscious. Like a puppet, your puppet.

You can hear her moan as you throw her onto the bed, tie her arms behind her and gag her mouth. Her legs hang over the side and you pull her panties off. She's shaved herself like a porn slut. It makes you hard. Pulling her bra up you can see her breasts are large, swollen. You'd like to suck her dark nipples but that'd leave trace and you're too smart, too restrained. Parting her legs wide you slide your sheathed cock in fast, making it hurt. Punishment should hurt if you want the change to make a lasting impact. One of the lessons Father taught you. Plus, you want her awake to feel you. Good. You can hear her breathe in sharply, frantically wriggling, but your weight holds her down. If only you could see her eyes. See the fear change to acceptance. She stops struggling. Has she accepted her fate? Or maybe she's enjoying the fuck, like the slut she is.

You tighten the cord some more until she's out again. You can't run the risk of anyone hearing the bitch screaming. Even with the gag in she'd make noise as you take care of the next part of your fix, especially as the walls are so fucking thin in these modern houses. All crammed so closely together your neighbours can hear you take a dump in the morning. But still, it has to be here as it's the only other place, next to the hospital, that she's been recently. You needed to make sure you wouldn't be spotted as completing the fix will take longer with this one. It's different. You won't enjoy it but it's necessary.

You open your Buck blade and make a long horizontal incision above the pubic bone, pushing in deep. She's whimpering so you need to tighten the cord again. You push your hand into the opening feeling around, just like the surgical YouTube videos show. There's nothing you can't learn to do these days online. There it is, it's the size of a lemon. You pull it out. It feels warm, alive. You cut the cord. You don't enjoy this bit but you want to protect this unborn entity from the pain that you endured. It's a kindness. You've saved it, really.

There's more blood than normal. Not what you'd expected. It takes you longer to make sure you've left no marks in the blood, no footprints, nothing. Everything is back in your pack. You'll burn it all later. When she wakes she will see your deed and have to live with the price of her immoral deeds. That's your gift. You make your call and slide out of the patio door into the already dark evening.

CHAPTER THIRTEEN

Ally

I really didn't think the day could progress any slower. It was only lunchtime and every second that passed felt more like an hour. It was the one thing about starting a relationship that I hated. Who makes the first move? How long after the first night of sex should you wait before you call? Too soon and you come across as pushy. Too long and it looks like you aren't interested. Were we even in a relationship? Argh, the dilemmas, I screamed in my head and decided a walk to the café for a sandwich could take up some more time.

'D' you guys want anything from the café'? What's up?' I asked seeing Sharon and Steph hunched over the appointments book.

'Oh, it's nothing. Looks like we had a no show. Maybe Anne didn't relay the message back to the client.' Sharon's oversized earrings moving in time with her head.

'Yeah, I guess that's likely. I'll call her after lunch, see what's happened,' Steph agreed.

'Who's this we're talking about? Is it a new

184

client . . . one of yours, Steph?'

'Ah, yeah. Anne Bishopton called on Tuesday to see if we could prioritise Karen Whitelaw. She'd seen Rev Proctor to see if her and Denise could come for couples counselling . . . y' know after the incident. Really it was to show support for Denise. But anyway, John felt it was beyond his scope, that they would be better here, so Anne made the referral. Anne said Karen wanted to come to the first session herself because she wanted some guidance on the best way to deal with Denise. It hasn't been easy. Denise isn't coping well with what's happened.'

'How come no one told me about this?'

'Well, you weren't in when she made the referral, or I'd have asked. And your appointments were full, so I thought Steph could take the referral. Was I wrong?'

'It's just that I've been handling these cases. But yeah, I know my appointments are pretty full on at the moment. Has anyone called Karen?'

'No, not yet. We were just going to call Anne, as I said.'

A wave of nausea swept over me. 'Bring up Karen's number, Sharon. Now.'

There was no answer from her house, and Denise's parents, at the hospital, confirmed that she wasn't there either when Sharon phoned round.

'Quick get Nick on the phone,' I shouted to Sharon, whose normally calm composure looked visibly shaken by my reaction.

There wasn't time for pleasantries as I quickly explained to Nick my concerns. And while he said he thought maybe I was being a bit paranoid, he agreed to send a car to Karen's house to check. Within twenty minutes of the call we watched as several sirens were heard passing through the town. I

185

cancelled my afternoon clients, which were thankfully people I'd been seeing for some time. They'd be fine missing one session.

I headed to Karen's house, worried about what I would find, sure I was about to confirm my gut suspicions of yet another rape. I don't know why I had the feeling, but I did. To me it was now obviously homophobic – even if Gill was the exception. However, if it was Bill Bishopton, then Gill fitted into the equation nicely. I just couldn't believe the police weren't doing more about it. Talking of which, I realised that I'd see Nick sooner than I thought I would. It was not the way I'd imagined our next romantic encounter.

Parkend Terrace had a police car blocking entry to the street so I parked a few streets away and walked. I showed my ID badge to the policeman at the boundary and asked for Nick or Jake. Within a few minutes another policeman was escorting me down the street to the gate of Denise and Karen's modern, terraced house. I noticed that the ambulance was still there, among several other police vehicles, just as Nick, wearing a white forensics suit, made an appearance from the front door. He touched my upper arm and I wondered if this was his way of showing affection to me in this chaotic situation.

'Nick, why is the ambulance still here? It's Karen, isn't it? She's been raped, too, hasn't she? What's happened? Why hasn't the ambulance left?' I knew I was bombarding him with questions. I didn't know what else to do.

'Ally.' Nick's brow was furrowed as he shook his head. 'It's not good, Ally.'

'What d'you mean? Tell me, Nick,' I pleaded.

'Karen Whitelaw is dead.'

'Dead? But . . . but she's pregnant. What about

the baby?' My hand rose to my mouth in horror, or trying to quell the rising bile from spilling out onto Nick's shoes.

'There was too much blood. It looks like a call to emergency services was made but her phone died before it connected. She bled out.'

'No, no. So now he's a murderer,' I stated angrily.

'That's not the worst of it.' Nick looked sick to his stomach. He glanced round to make sure no one was within earshot. 'The foetus was cut out of her and left on her stomach to die, also.'

'So even if she'd survived, her baby wouldn't've,' I acknowledged unwillingly.

'Look, I need to go – that's CID arrived, they'll want to be briefed. I'll try and call later, okay?' He smiled weakly as he left to talk to CID while I stood grimly watching the forensic team setting up their tents over the front door and the police securing the perimeter. A full scale investigation would be carried out, but I knew the murderer wouldn't have left any evidence. He was too smart. As I wondered how we would stop this monster, someone called my name. It was Jake.

'Ally, I need to go to the hospital to tell Denise before she hears about it on the news. Will you come with me? I think it'd be best if you were there to assist in the fall out.'

'Of course. Anything,' I said, relieved to be of use. 'I left my car a few streets down.'

'I'll run you to it.'

As I climbed into Jake's car I noticed Nick watching. I hoped he wouldn't interpret it in the wrong way, but then again, maybe I was putting too much into the whole relationship thing.

The news of Karen's murder was, as expected, not taken well by Denise. It was just as well she was still in her bed as she collapsed into the arms of her mother, when Jake broke it to her. When she came to, she was so distraught, the nurses had to give her something to calm her down before she hurt herself. I knew I'd need to stay a while to help her and her family deal with the news. But before Jake left I had to ask him about Bill Bishopton.

'Doesn't this clarify that the perp is targeting gays, Jake?'

'Maybe,' he answered reluctantly.

'I take it you'll ask Bill and Anne where they were last night? Especially as it was Anne that made Karen's referral to the centre. That's too much of a coincidence. Don't you think?'

'Maybe. Look Ally, you're doing it again – interfering. You've got to stop. Of course we'll check this out. It's where I'm headed next,' he argued defensively.

'Everyone knows he's dangerous. Hell, even someone at the gay demo told my sister how Bishopton had tried to strangle his own daughter in a fit of rage when he found out she was gay. They haven't spoken since. As for Gill, not fitting the MO, well, she reported Bishopton to the police so there's plenty of motive there.'

'He tried to strangle his daughter? We didn't know that. I've got to go Ally. And anyway, it looks like Denise is coming around.'

I stayed for several hours, trying to manage the grief that Denise and her family felt. It was like trying to stop the contents of a boiling pot with a lid on from spilling all over the hob, it couldn't be done. Support was the key when everything you ever cared about was gone. I'd seen it so many times in my career to know that you could only really hold someone's hand but the journey was theirs to make.

I felt bone weary as I left the hospital, pulling my coat around me closer in an attempt to ward off the freezing wind blowing across the exposed car park. As I got to my car, I saw Nick coming out of the hospital. He smiled warmly to the woman at his side as she moved closer, putting her arm through his. It was an act of closeness. I felt sick as I watched. It was the same woman I'd seen in his office. She was small and slim, blonde hair framing a pretty face. They walked together to Nick's car, parked close to the entrance, and he opened the car door for her.

Who the fuck was she? Was Nick Daniels a fucking cheat? I despised cheats. Luckily none of my previous relationships had ever ended because of infidelity, but I knew first-hand from my clients, the damage done in a relationship when a partner was unfaithful, and it was not something I wanted to experience personally. I watched as they drove away, resisting the urge to follow. I would not be that person, even though it took every inch of my being.

I drove home reluctantly and made myself some dinner. After pushing some salad around my plate until it resembled a pathetic, wilted image of its former self, I gave up and turned to a packet of chocolate biscuits instead for some comfort. My mind was racing with thoughts of Karen, the other rapes and Nick. I was torturing myself. He said he'd phone later. I wondered if that was before or after he would fuck blondie.

I lit some candles and added some lavender to a warm bath to soak away my worries, but five minutes in and my doorbell rang. Dripping all over the doormat I looked through the peephole to see Nick standing on the doorstep. My stomach lurched. I thought he was otherwise engaged.

'Nick, I . . . I didn't expect you.'

'No, I see that.' His gaze rolled over me, taking in my skimpy wrap stuck to my wet body. 'You look good, you smell good,' he said into my ear as he put an arm round my waist, pulling me close and breathing in my scent.

'Nick? I need to ask you something,' I said pulling back.

'God, please, Ally, not the investigation. Later. I can't think about that now.'

'Nick, I saw you with a woman today . . . at the hospital. You looked close. And I've seen you with her before, at the station. Who is she, Nick? I don't do the whole mistress thing. It's not me.'

'Christ. What d'you take me for. Is that what you think?' He looked angry. Disappointed, even. Was I wrong? He hesitated. 'It's my wife, but look, it's not like that.'

'What? *Your wife?* Are you kidding me?'

'It's not what you think. We're separated. We have been for a year, but her mother is dying and she doesn't know that we split. So I go with her sometimes to the hospital. Libby, my wi– ex-wife, doesn't want to upset her, and I'm okay with that. Not every relationship ends in hate, you know.'

I did know. My own relationship had ended amicably too. I felt like a fool for being jealous and presumptuous. 'So, you're doing it to protect an old dying woman?' I approached him and pulled him against my wet body, allowing the wrap to fall open.

'Yep. See, I really am a good guy,' he said huskily, as he grabbed my arse and lowered his mouth to my nipple.

190

My mobile vibrated and rang loudly against my bedside table, rousing me from sleep. I shifted from under Nick's arm to pick it up and answer, unsure of what time it was.

'Ally, it's Jinny. Can you please come? Come now. It's Charley. She's in a state. I don't know what to do.' Jinny sounded frantic on the other end of the call.

'What's happened?' I questioned, trying to figure out what needed to be done. I could feel Nick stirring next to me and he raised himself up on one arm to listen in.

'She just woke up, screaming. She's hysterical. She's in the corner of the room crying. She won't come out and I can't get her to calm down.'

'I'm on my way,' I said reassuringly. It was 3.30 am, no wonder I felt dazed.

I explained to Nick what the call was about and got dressed hurriedly. He dressed, too, saying he'd drive. I was glad he was with me and as he drove I gave him some background information on Charley. I knew she wouldn't mind; as the police knew about her past.

'Rape or abuse. That's all I hear about these days. What sort of world have we humans created?' He sounded despondent.

'I know. I think that, too. It really brings me down some days, after dealing with all the trauma clients have been through.' He placed his hand on my leg and I put my hand over his and squeezed it gently. 'Us against the world, eh?'

***

191

Ally called Gill as Nick drove, asking her to go to Jinny's as well. Getting a house visit these days was near impossible unless you were practically comatose, but she knew Gill would do it as a personal favour, and Gill agreed that Charley would likely need a sedative. With the streets empty because it was so early, and Nick driving faster than the speed limit, they got to Jinny's pretty fast. Ally had her own key for the place. They bolted up the stairs to find Charley wrapped in Jinny's arms on the bedroom sofa. She was gently rocking her as she stroked her hair.

'She's calm now. I managed to coax her out of the corner, and told her you were on your way to help, which seemed to do the trick.'

Charley lifted her head and nodded in agreement. 'I'm sorry. I didn't mean to cause any trouble. And I didn't mean for you to get the police either.' Charley looked at Nick and Ally, seeming embarrassed at the hassle she thought she'd caused.

'No, honey. You didn't cause any trouble. Nick was with me anyway. He wanted to come to help. I told him a wee bit about you. I hope that was okay?'

'Hmm,' she replied. 'Still, I'm sorry. It's the middle of the night. I woke up in a panic. I've started to remember things, Ally. Snippets. Just like you said would happen. It scared me. Why now, Ally?'

'It's completely normal for anyone with repressed memories. Sometimes the memories come in flashes, other times it might be a smell or seeing something familiar that lets fragments of the memory leak back into your consciousness. And for some it's when they've let go of trying to remember. Maybe because they feel safe to let the memory return.'

'Yeah, 'cause I feel happy now, relaxed, with Jinny,' Charley said, moving her head closer to Jinny, who pulled her in tighter.

'What was the flashback, Charley? If you don't mind telling us, of course,' Nick asked, interested in what was happening.

'It was more like a dream, but when I woke up I could still feel it, and more images came to mind. I dreamt I was sleeping, but in the dream I woke up and I was suffocating. There was something over my head. I . . . I couldn't see or breathe. And then . . . well, you know.' She looked at Ally. 'He was . . . you know?' She choked a little and Jinny held a class of water for her while she took a drink.

'It's okay, Charley. You're saying you remember now, yeah?'

Charley nodded and closed her eyes, tears leaking out as she huddled in tight to Jinny's chest.

'Take your time. We're all here to protect you,' Nick said comfortingly. Ally smiled at him, glad that he was helping. 'You said something was over your head?' Nick looked at Ally. No one apart from those involved in the investigation knew that the current victims all had something covering their head, so Charley wasn't unconsciously adding anything that she'd heard from the media.

'Yeah, I couldn't see anything. It was like a bag with a string around my neck. That was what was choking me. I couldn't remember anything after that.' Charley looked up. 'But now, hearing about that poor woman being murdered . . . Oh, I'm scared he'll come after me or Jinny. The news is saying that this person is attacking gay women. They showed Bill Bishopton being arrested, being taken away by the police.' Charley looked as though she was becoming agitated again and Ally could tell from Nick's reaction that they both had suspicions – that Charley was an early victim of the same perpetrator.

Jinny shushed her and kissed her head, holding her close. 'Don't worry Charley, I remember my karate from years back. I'll kick the fuck out of anyone that tries. I promise.'

Charley touched Jinny's face and smiled up at her before closing her eyes and tucking her head back in under Jinny's chin.

'Nick, can I speak with you?' Ally nodded in the direction of the hall, where they could speak in private. 'You're thinking what I'm thinking, aren't you?' she said immediately. 'I didn't connect Charley's rape to these ones because it was a while ago and she's never said anything about something over her head before, choking her. It's a similar MO. Nick, Charley's attacker raped her and messed her up internally, with a hairbrush. We said that the attacker may have escalated and refined his actions over the years.' Ally knew she was right and looking at Nick's face told her he agreed.

'Did Bishopton know Charley back then? She was quite young,' he questioned.

'Yep. Jinny told me what Charley said after the demo. Bill Bishopton was in the same year as her brother, John – you know, the minister. Charley said Bill was a bully, the worst kind. Name-calling, humiliating other kids. He was a nasty little shit and he had a thing against gay people back then, she said. He used to bully John, too, although I'm not sure why, he's not gay, but bullies like Bishopton will pick on anyone, right?'

'Ally, I think I need to get to the station. I'll call Jake in. We'll look deeper into Bishopton and further back. And before I forget, we're still looking at Hargreaves.' Ally looked at him questioningly. 'All I can say just now is it seems like the mayor may have called in a few favours to protect his son.'

'Now there's a surprise. Nick, I don't want you to go.'

'I know. But I have to. I'll text you later.' He drew her close, kissing her deeply, then reluctantly opened the door to leave.

'Will you get back okay? Take a cab?'

'I'll probably just crash here. Jinny'll run me back in the morning.'

He nodded. Gill arrived as he was going out the door. Another one who looked tired. Ally showed her in to the living room and explained what had happened. Thankfully Gill was aware of Charley's medical history, so with Charley's approval, it didn't take much for her to administer the sedative.

Gill didn't stay longer than necessary, explaining that she hoped to grab some more sleep before her alarm clock was due to go off. But Ally felt something was bothering her. 'Thanks for coming, Gill, we really appreciate your help,' she said, seeing the GP out to the hallway while Jinny put Charley back to bed. 'Is something up? You look worried.'

'I'm just tired. It's been a long week. Maybe I should've taken longer off work.'

'Are you sure that's all? You know you can talk to me at any time. You've been through so much.'

'I'm fine, Ally. Really, I am. Don't worry about me,' Gill replied trying to sound convincing, but Ally wasn't convinced. 'You want a run home?'

Noting Gill's quick subject change, Ally thought it was probably for the best to get that lift home. Charley was settled, and Jinny was looking after her. 'That'd be great, thanks. I'll just run up and let Jinny know. Get you at the car.' Ally wondered if Gill would say any more on their way home. Unlikely, but she wasn't going to miss the opportunity.

***

Jinny

The sun was gently warming my bedroom as I slowly opened my eyes. I stayed still, watching shadows of the trees dancing on the wall while I mentally tried to make recognisable shapes out of the patterns. I was enjoying the cosy peacefulness of the moment, trying to not make any sudden moves that might waken Charley. She was nestled into me, the arm holding her to me feeling quite numb. I tried to move my hand to get circulation back but Charley stirred as I lifted my hand off, so I put it back again.

'I'm awake. But I'm so cosy here.'

'You okay?'

'Ah-hah. A bit fuzzy from the sedative. But otherwise, I'm good.'

'Thank God. You scared me shitless last night.'

'Scared me too, but today, in the daylight, I'm good. More than good.' Charley's hand slid into my shorts and found my wetness. I was afraid last night's memories might have set her back, us back, but she seemed to . . . well, I wasn't sure if I should retaliate, until she looked into my eyes and smiled before covering my mouth with hers. How come morning breath wasn't a problem when you kissed? I never understood that as my tongue returned the explorations. My not-numb hand felt its way under her top and she moaned as I peaked her nipples with my teasing. I very gingerly eased down her body, ready to pull back if she showed any hesitation at all. She didn't. She pushed her fingers deeper into me as my fingers entered her, kissing me deeper and moaning in delight as my thumb found her clitoris. We climaxed together, letting our mouths part for air.

196

'Jinny?'

'Yeah?'

'Oh God, how do I say this, but . . .'

'You okay?' I was worried. Had she still issues from her memories? Maybe I got carried away, should have given her more time, no matter how willing she seemed?

'Oh I'm more than okay, but . . . Fuck it, I'm just going to say it. I love you. I fucking love you.'

I felt emotional as she spoke. She looked so proud of her outburst, so confident. This was the real Charley; she'd found herself from before the rape. And I fucking loved her right back, I told her.

'I was worried your memories would . . . you know . . .'

'So was I, last night. But when I woke next to you, knowing I love you so much that I want to explore every part of you in every way, and you to do the same to me, I knew. I just bloody knew that what happened to me was so different and in no way would it ever impact on how I feel about you, about us. This is so tender, it's so wonderful.'

'Charley Proctor, you are amazing. I want to be with you forever.'

'I was so terrified you wouldn't love me back. Oh my God, I'm so lucky.'

'You kidding? I'm the fucking lucky one.'

'Y' know what? I'm so fucking glad you left your phone downstairs. I'm getting as bad as you.'

We laughed so hard tears were streaming down our faces as we both imagined my phone pinging away loudly.

***

Charley and I arrived together at the coven. Amira

197

noticed but didn't say anything. Everyone else seemed to be so concerned about Karen's murder that there was a solemnness in the room that was in contrast to the normally positive atmosphere.

'It's like a wake tonight. It feels like everyone's in mourning,' Charley whispered in my ear.

'I know. The sadness is palpable,' I returned quietly, since everyone else in the room was silent.

Amira clapped her hands and her bangles made a melodic jingle, which seemed out of place. 'Let's sit in a circle and spend a few minutes sending healing love to Denise and Karen's family who are in mourning.'

Everyone eagerly found a cushion on the floor and sat cross-legged on it. Charley sat beside Amira, I stayed next to Charley, and Debbie was on my other side.

'Ally not coming tonight?' Debbie enquired.

'I think she's helping the police with the case,' I told her.

'Of course. Poor Ally. This must be so intense for her.'

'It is. She does her best though.'

'You two must be close. I bet you're a great support to her.'

'We're good for each other,' I agreed.

'Right.' Amira called us to attention. 'Let's close our eyes, join hands and ask our spirit guides for protection.'

Everyone carried out the same ritual of calling on our guides to protect us and guide us. Amira then said a prayer for Denise, asking the spirit world to ease her grief and to give Karen and her baby peace in their time of rest in the place beyond. Everyone then spent a few moments in silent prayer, mainly giving people time for any of their own religious preferences of prayer.

'Okay, thank you for that. I felt the warmth of your love through our circle,' Amira said. We all brought our hands back to our laps. 'I think tonight would be appropriate to look at stronger methods of self-protection. While the town protection worked indirectly, it still left individuals unprotected. I know a few of you have asked how you can protect yourselves, your family and your home.' There were positive mumblings around the circle. 'Nasir and I have come up with a few ideas that can help. Nasir?'

'Yes. I think it would be good to do a spell for protection, where we ask our inner God or Goddess to give us strength to protect ourselves. Then we will each choose a protection crystal and charge it with positive protective energy.' Debbie put up her hand quickly. 'Yes Debbie?'

'Can I have a crystal for my sister?'

'Certainly. There are plenty here. If anyone else wants to take extra for family members, please do.'

Charley nudged me and mouthed, 'Ally?' I smiled at her thoughtfulness for my sister and nodded.

Amira was talking now. 'The Goddess of protection spell came from the premise that Hecate was a dark Goddess and protector of witches. Spell books have adapted the spell to suit their own needs and beliefs. Nasir and I look at it more as a call on our own inner strength and wisdom to help us be aware and wise in our responses to keep ourselves safe. So we have adapted the spell accordingly.'

'Who was Hecate?' Robert asked.

Amira answered, 'Hecate was considered as the ruler of heaven, earth and the underworld by Greek mythology. She was considered to be the Goddess of witchcraft. And that's why she is used in spells of protection. I have lots of books on her in the library. Please feel free to borrow them.' Robert nodded, satisfied.

'Always fancied a peek in their library,' I admitted to Charley.

'Oh yes. Let's make a night of it sometime.'

'And for the home,' Amira continued, 'we will use the old traditional method of using a rope of garlic. Garlic has been known for centuries for its protective affects against the evil of maladies, from pest infestations and from evil spirits. It's been used in spells to keep vampires away, to protect against bad weather, and to enhance strength and power. We can see where the benefits hail from scientifically, as garlic is a natural antibacterial and antifungal, and certainly it's pungent enough to keep some people away.' Everyone laughed and nodded. Nasir breathed into his cupped hand and nodded to everyone to prove its potency. Amira continued, 'So we have lovely strings of garlic for you all to take home and yes, extra, Debbie,' she added quickly as she saw Debbie start to raise her hand. 'So let's prepare for the spell first and then we will work on choosing and protecting our crystals. And we will hand you all out the garlic as you leave. How does that sound?'

Everybody agreed in some fashion. Nasir went around the outer circle of where we sat, placed candles and lit them. He then lifted the rug we were all sitting around to reveal their pentagram. The pentagram itself was marked with dark shades of wooden parquet set within the flooring's lighter parquet tiles. Nasir placed the main candle in the middle and lit it, then went back to his cushion. He nodded to Amira that they were ready to begin. As always, Amira started with calling on our guides to protect us and then started on the spell. We all held hands and closed our eyes as she said one line and then we repeated it:

'We call upon our inner strength,
Our wisdom and our guides
To protect us with an aura
On the inside and outside
To protect us in a golden egg
That reflects negative energy out
The lets positive energy in
And feeds inner strength
And takes away our doubt.
And when in times of fear
Or in times of strife
We can free our inner God or Goddess
To protect our precious life.
Trust in our inner God or Goddess
To protect our precious life.'

Eyes still closed, we kept repeating the last two lines as Nasir went around the outer circle blowing out the candles. As he got to the middle one he raised his voice so we knew that was the final incantation, and he ended it by blowing out the final candle. We opened our eyes slowly and let each other's hands go. Charley squeezed mine and smiled before she did. I felt warm and fuzzy inside as I smiled back. Amira clapped her hands to get our attention, and her bangles jangled.

'Okay, everyone, let's break for refreshments before my bum goes numb.' Everyone laughed. Mine was already numb. 'Then we will choose our protection crystals.'

We all moved through to the kitchen area and helped ourselves to the usual delicacies of raw delights – for which I still needed to get the recipes. As Amira was standing beside me, now was as good a time as any to ask.

'Amira, I've been dying to ask you for the recipes for these. Would you mind if I copied them and sold them in my café?'

'Jinny, I'd be honoured if you did. In fact, I run dessert workshops regularly. Why don't you come to one? Bring your staff too.'

'That would be perfect. Thanks.'

'I'll email you the dates of the next one.'

Debbie chimed in, 'Could you email me, too? I'd love to know how to make these.'

'I'll let you all know. Now I'd better go and get some more out since they're disappearing fast.' Amira excused herself and rushed to the fridge.

After some chat, the atmosphere was much more positive than when we'd arrived. Everyone probably felt more empowered, which was all you could hope for when you felt vulnerable and out of control.

'I enjoyed that spell,' Charley admitted. 'I'm going to ask Amira for a copy of it so I can say it to myself.'

'Good idea. We can do it together.'

'Yeah.'

Before we knew it, Nasir was calling us all over to a table of glass bowls, all filled with a selection of shaped and coloured gemstones. I had no idea what they were but Nasir was holding up a leaflet for us to take – after we'd chosen our crystal. He wanted us to choose first because we would be drawn to the one we specifically needed. One by one, we were to hold our hands over the bowls; if we took our time to pick them up and feel them, he said, we'd know the right one for us. I doubted that. I looked at Charley, but she was entranced, so I kept my mocking trap shut. When Debbie asked how to choose one for someone else, Nasir told her just to constantly hold the image of the person in their mind's eye and repeat the same process. Charley looked at me and whispered, 'You can do that for Ally.' I nodded as my heart skipped a beat. God, I loved this woman.

It took about fifteen minutes until I got my shot. Charley went before me and came back smiling, and putting an orangey-red stone into the metal spiral holding cage that Nasir gave her. She fed that onto the blue ribbon she'd chosen and tied it round her neck, all before examining the leaflet to find out *what* she'd chosen. I made my way to the table.

This feels silly.

Really, how was I going to know which was mine? Maybe I should just pretend to feel attracted to one. As I waved my hand over the dishes, I was visually attracted to a dish filled with smooth colourful stones. I rummaged through them, noticing a particularly colourful one: blues, greens, pinks, purples and clear. It was warm in my hand and, I'm sure it was my imagination, but it felt like it was getting even warmer. I placed it down and picked up another. It didn't feel as warm and didn't get warmer. I put that one down and picked up the one I liked. Yep, it was warm. I guessed this was what Nasir meant.

I put mine aside and thought of Ally. I saw her in my mind and said her name to myself three times. Nasir hadn't said to do that, but I liked the idea of it. It felt right. Maybe I'd read too many paranormal books but I felt primed now to pick Ally's stone. I ran my hands over the bowls and was drawn to a really black stone, which surprised me. Why would I choose a black stone for Ally who, in my mind, suffered from dark moods, thanks to the job she was in? I looked around at the other stones. There was a purple one, which I presumed was amethyst. I was sure that was more Ally's stone. I had no idea what amethyst was for but I lifted one up and felt it. It was cold and I didn't really feel anything for it. I was still drawn to the black one. Damn. I picked up another gem – too cool – then a few more until one of those felt warm. I gave in to my intuition and settled on the black one for Ally. I chose a purple ribbon for her and a blue one for me, and collected two of the information leaflets, then went back to sit on the floor beside Charley.

'What did you get?' she asked before my bum hit the cushion. 'Mine is fire agate, and listen to this, 'fire agate has a calming vibration, bringing feelings of security and safety. It creates a shield around the wearer, protecting them from negative energies, returning the harm back to the source, so the source learns the effects of their intended harm. It helps with analysing inner emotions and uncovering hidden trauma and heals the wearer, giving them courage to start over and foster love'. Oh my God. That's just me, isn't it? How amazing is that?'

'Fu– Fantastic!'

'I see what you did there. Come on, what did you choose? It's lovely. Look at the colours in it.'

'Yeah, it was the colours that attracted me.' I felt stupid admitting there was something esoteric about my decision-making, so I kept that aspect to myself. 'I just really liked this one.'

'Look.' Charley showed me the picture on the chart. 'It's a fluorite. Says here, oh my God, Jinny, it says here it's great 'for shielding against computer and electromagnetic stress, stabilises the emotions' – hey, that'll help your swearing, ha! – and is good for balance in relationships. Can you believe that?'

I couldn't. I read my own leaflet and, fuck me, it did say that. 'I'm speechless. Seriously, this is spooky as hell, Charl.'

'Tell me about it. I was freaked by mine, but now I'm more freaked by yours. What did you get for Ally?'

I searched the leaflet. 'Black obsidian. "A powerful cleanser of negative energies, cuts through blockages and protects the wearer from negative energy." Wow, Ally could certainly do with that when she's at work. Listen, it also says it grounds a person, enhances powers of discernment and prophecy, and prevents mental stress and tension.'

'Well done on that pick, Jin. That's just perfect for Ally.'

Both of us were pretty freaked out by our choices. We also took the garlic strings offered on the way out, and by then, if Amira had handed me a broom and told me I could fly home, I'd have ditched the car and hopped on it.

***

Ally

Usually, I enjoyed Saturday mornings. Lazy mornings, taking time over breakfast and reading the morning news. Not this Saturday. I tossed and turned, eventually throwing the duvet off and getting up early. I scoured the news channels and discovered the usual news about the latest terror attacks, austerity driving people to suicide, another politician accused of fondling his assistant's breast and the latest health risk scaremongering. This month it was prostate cancer, last month cervical cancer. Yep, the usual smorgasbord of fear, corruption and propaganda. There was nothing new on the rapes or murder. I sighed. When would we see an end to the terror lurking in our own neighbourhood? My thoughts ran to Charley and then Nick. I knew he'd be busy looking into Bill Bishopton's past and his alibis for each of the cases. And now Simon Hargreaves too.

The doorbell interrupted my thoughts. I looked through the peephole to see Gill Garby standing on the step looking nervous.

'Gill. I didn't expect to see you. Come on in.'

'Sorry it's early, Ally. I wasn't sure if you had any plans this weekend. I wanted to catch you before you went out,' she explained.

'No, please come in. I was just looking at the news and contemplating going for a run later in the morning.' I guided her into the kitchen area and made some more coffee while she planted herself at the breakfast bar.

'I lied to you last night . . . about being alright,' she said, waiting on my reprisal.

'I know. But if you didn't want to tell me, then maybe it's none of my business.'

'It's about the rapes. I just had to piece it together. Y' know, in my mind.' She took a sip of coffee, stalling, or maybe just gathering her thoughts. I didn't want to rush her. 'My friend was raped. It was years ago. Maybe about a year after Charley's attack.'

'You've been thinking about her because of all the current goings on, and what happened to you?' I admired her courage after what she had been through. I wondered if I'd be as strong.

'No. Well, yes, in a way. I'd been thinking about what'd happened to me, and it got me thinking about my friend, Chrissie – Chrissie Sims. It was so long ago I hadn't really thought much about it. I was a young woman and shocked at what had happened but I only saw her once after she was raped, which I feel bad about now. But before the rape, we were at uni in the

206

city. It wasn't far from here, but we felt so grown up.'

'Go on.'

'Chrissie and I were on different courses; she did law and had a flat with friends, whereas I was in a room at student accommodation, so we drifted apart, as you do. She got raped one evening near the student union bar. I think she was going to meet some friends and never showed up. When I heard what'd happened I asked my mum to come with me to see her at the hospital and I overheard her mum telling mine that Chrissie would never be a mother, she had had to have surgery. That was all I overheard, and Chrissie never said a thing about it.'

'Surgery? So, what're you thinking Gill? That your friend had something similar happen to her, like you and the other victims?' My mind was racing. Rape was a horrific crime but to mutilate the victim too, was pretty rare – or so I once believed. 'Can you contact Chrissie, ask her what happened?'

'I can't contact her. She committed suicide two years after the rape. She couldn't handle it; the looks and gossiping about her. I remember how frightened she looked in hospital. I've wondered recently if that was how people saw me too. I think that's why I just wanted to get on, get back to work. So that people wouldn't see me like that.'

'Oh God, I'm sorry Gill.' I put my hand over hers. 'No one thinks like that. Really. Everyone admires you, your courage.'

'I just didn't want the pity, or for people to see me as different, as they did with Chrissie. I know now that it was because she carried it about with her, never getting over it. That attracted the pity. It's such a waste.'

'Does she have any family?'

'I've already spoken to her mother. She's pretty

old now but her memory's as sharp as a pin. She remembered me, and all the events back then. She was livid because at first everyone just assumed Chrissie was drunk, asking for it. She said the campus police reported they saw rapes all the time and many of them were girls that woke up the next day, after a drunken night out, regretting their actions.'

'Appalling, isn't it? So many women not listened to, not believed and blamed.' The anger rose in me for all women that had been through this.

'It's worse than that, Ally. Her mother said Chrissie was raped and then a screwdriver was used to tear up her insides. The police believed the perpetrator tried to strangle her, because she had ligature marks on her neck, but he must have been interrupted, or thought he was going to be seen, so he fled. Chrissie called an ambulance before falling unconscious, otherwise she would've died in the bushes a few feet away from the bar where all her friends were waiting for her. The university didn't want the news of it affecting their intake rates, so they leaned on the police to stop their investigation and it was quickly hushed up.'

'Even though they thought it was an attempted murder? That's shocking.'

'Yep. And it's the same, Ally, isn't it? It's the same type of attack,' she stated.

We both knew what that could mean – this person may have been active for a long time.

'Even the phone call got me thinking,' she went on. 'No one at the time questioned how she managed to make that phone call when she was found quite a distance from any phone box.'

'We need to let Nick know about this. It might assist with the timeline of events and help them to track the person that's doing this. Nick said he's looking into Bishopton's past, after what Charley told him. What do you remember of Bill back then?'

'Bill was exactly the bully that Charley described. And he was like that all through school and beyond. There were a few of us that left high school and went to uni and he was one of them. I couldn't tell you what course he did though, as I stayed away from him. And as far as I can remember he never graduated. He met Anne and went off to Spain for a while until his parents retired.'

'Still the bully. Poor Anne. I don't think business has been good for the pub since this all kicked off,' I replied, thinking back to the demo outside the hotel.

'There's something else, Ally. I've never spoken about it before. It was never important as it was past history.' Gill shifted uncomfortably on her stool.

'Is it important to the investigation?' I questioned.

'I'm not sure . . . but, yeah, probably. I . . . I had a brief relationship with Chrissie. Well, it was more like experimentation. We were young women, just left school, just started university.' Gill's face was red but she carried on.

'We did some netball coaching at the local school. It helped us stay in touch with each other and well . . . we were having fun.' She looked uneasy as she recalled the past.

'There's nothing to be embarrassed about. Lots of people try out various relationships when they're young. It's pretty common nowadays,' I was trying to make her feel more at ease.

'Oh, I know. It's just that I've never told anyone, not even Steve. Probably because it wasn't so common when we were young. I mean, it only lasted a month or so. I never felt quite comfortable – I guess

I came to realise I was straight, end of. It just dawned on me that maybe that was why Bill targeted me, because of that relationship, and not because I'd reported him to the police about his wife beating. I just didn't think anyone knew about it. I never told anyone. But he would harass me to go out with him and I know Chrissie had words with him . . .' Gill looked confused but she was right, I thought, maybe that was the real reason Bishopton had a problem with Gill, not just that she had reported him to the police.

'Maybe Chrissie told him I was with her. She was always so forthright about her sexuality.'

'I guess we'll never know,' I surmised.

'Do you want to call Nick, or shall I?' Gill asked, sounding stronger.

CHAPTER FOURTEEN

They're telling lies about you on the news on the television. Their twisted, manipulated fake news. You're doing all you can to stop yourself from raging. To stop yourself from screaming at the top of your lungs that you are no murderer. Not you. They have it wrong. You don't murder. You save. You fix.

It wasn't your fault that her phone died and she bled out. That wasn't supposed to happen. She'll never be fixed. She'll never know the beauty of the gift you gave her. As for the unborn, you saved it from a life of harm and evil. It will never endure what you did. Your work should be seen as heroic, not this, not what they are saying.

Their words stab into your head like knives. They remind you of your parents' words, that as a child you couldn't understand.

Evil, unclean, spawn of the devil and the whore that created you.

You hid in the cupboard, but they found you to punish and teach you. You learned the right way. The way that you now teach, through your punishments. This was not your mistake.

The media celebrate these abominations. Gay

and transgender rights. Political correctness. Watch every word you say or someone will be offended. Schools teaching debauchery to innocent children, brainwashing them into accepting these perversions are normal. They will come to see that you are right. That this moral degradation of society will be short-lived. It will take time for them to catch up to your work, but they will, and they'll see the error in their ways.

CHAPTER FIFTEEN

Jinny could feel her old skills coming back quickly as she practised her defence moves on Jake. There was definitely something to be said for muscle memory.

'I think you put a few moves in there of your own,' Jake acknowledged. 'Right Charley, your turn,' he said as he grabbed her in a neck hold.

Charley got out of the hold the way Jake had shown her, and Jinny felt proud watching her. Charley's confidence was growing day by day and it was even obvious in the way she handled Jake. Ever since her memory of the rape had returned, Jinny was worried it would set Charley back, but instead it seemed to have freed her, released her from her fear. She even winked at Jinny as she tackled Jake again. Trying not to laugh, Jinny caught sight of Ally and Nick sparring. They looked good together, and obviously intimate in the way they manhandled each other, as if they were enjoying themselves.

The class instructor calling an end to the session broke into Jinny's thoughts. She went over to Charley and they smiled at each other knowingly. 'Let's do this, eh?'

Charley nodded. 'I can't wait to see her face.'

'Me too.'

Linking arms, they grabbed their bags and headed to Ally who was gathering up her towel and protective hand mitts into her holdall. She turned quickly as they approached.

'Good reaction, sis,' Jinny joked, punching her sister playfully on her shoulder.

'What're you two looking so smug about?'

Jinny and Charley looked at each other. Jinny nodded to Charley.

'Jinny and I want you to be the first to know that I've moved in with Jinny.'

'That's great–'

'And we're going to get married,' Charley interrupted Ally to deliver the news.

Ally's mouth dropped open, then she grinned at them, grabbing them both into a hug.

'You guys. I'm really, really happy for you.'

Jinny let out her breath, 'You really mean it? You're not going to tell us we're moving too fast?'

Ally shook her head smiling. 'It's pretty obvious you're in love and well suited to each other. I'm happy for you both.'

'Well, we're not going to drag our heels on this. We want to do it as soon as there's a slot.' Jinny waited to see if Ally's face showed any signs of disapproval and was relieved to see her continue to smile at them.

Charley added quickly, 'We want you as bridesmaid.'

'Oh, I do hope so. I love weddings. Mum and Dad will be so pleased. When will you tell them, Jin?'

'I'll phone them tomorrow before we go see John and break the news to him,' Charley nodded as Jinny continued. 'So we have a date that suits them and can see if John can fit us in.'

'I think John will be shocked, but I'm sure he'll be relieved that he doesn't have to worry about me, or feel he needs to protect me. I feel I can protect myself now, and with Jinny I'm who I was meant to be.' Jinny pulled Charley into a tight hug, and then Ally too.

'Right,' Ally pulled away, tears in her eyes. 'I'll let you two get home. I've got things to do tonight.' Ally nodded her head in Nick's direction.

'At this rate maybe it'll be a double wedding,' Jinny teased.

'Oh no. I like to go slow. You know me.'

'Well, whatever you do, enjoy yourself. It's time you deserved some happiness, sis.'

'I intend to. Which reminds me, I'm seeing Nick tomorrow so I won't be at the coven. In fact, I don't think I'll be back. It's really not for me.'

'Ally, don't worry. We get it,' Charley told her. 'We'll go together, Jinny and I. Now Simon's not there it has a lovely atmosphere.'

'That's fine. As long as you don't go off on your own.'

'No chance of that. We've not been out each other's sight at all. I've even volunteered at the refuge while Charley's been there working. It's an eye opener. Makes me grateful for what we've got.'

'You guys . . .' Ally opened her arms and they all hugged again.

'Got something for you, sis,' Jinny said, pulling out of the hug and searching through her bag. She pulled out the gemstone necklace and put it over Ally's head. 'This is a charm we got for you from the coven. It protects you from negative sh– stuff. There's a leaflet explaining it in here.' Jinny pulled out a plastic bag; even though it was tightly knotted it was still pungent.

'I love the charm, but what the hell is the garlic stench?'

'Garlic protects your home,' Charley said quickly. 'So the charm is for you and the garlic is for your house.'

'Yay. How can I not accept that?' Ally quickly shoved it into her bag. 'Thank you. Now go, you two. And have a nice evening.'

'You too, sis,' Jinny replied, watching Ally head over to Nick. He put his arm around her and grabbed her bag with his other. Jinny had a good feeling about Nick.

'Home then?'

'Oh yes.' Charley smiled. 'Home, it is.'

***

Ally

I'd been quiet for most of the journey back to the cottage.

'You okay?'

Nick's question interrupted my thoughts. He looked concerned.

'What? Er, yeah. I'm just thinking about Jinny and Charley. They want to get married.'

'Really? And you're worried it's too soon, right?'

'Am I so transparent?'

'No, but I know that you want the best for both of them. And it does seem early in their relationship to be making long term plans.'

'It is, isn't it? But they both look so happy. I don't want to spoil that, I just want what's best for them both. I guess I worry they're rushing things because they both want a bit of stability in their lives.

I don't want them getting ahead of themselves before they get to know each other first.'

'They're grownups, Ally, they get to make their own fuck ups, remember?' Nick smiled warmly as he teased me.

'You're right. It's not up to me. I guess I'm not a spur of the moment type gal. I'm too used to taking time to think over big decisions, but that doesn't mean I always find the right outcome. I'm sure Jinny and Charley will convince me otherwise. I told them I was happy for them anyway.'

As Nick parked outside the cottage I wondered if I'd be making long term plans with him one day or were we just having a good time while it lasted? Maybe the investigation was the only thing we had in common – oh, and lust. He leaned over in his seat to kiss me.

'Bloody hell, Ally, have you been munching down on garlic bread? The smell of garlic would knock you down at a hundred feet away,' he said reeling back.

'Oh God, sorry Nick. Jinny and Charley gave me a rope of garlic tonight. I must be nose-blind to the smell now.' I laughed.

'Rope of garlic? What the hell? Y' know what? Don't tell me, those two are bloody crazy. C' mere though, I wanna go nose-blind as well,' he said tugging on my coat to pull me closer.

We made love in the shower and continued in the bedroom, our wet bodies glistening in the moonlight which cut across the bed. When we were spent, we lay in silence, our legs entwined and my hand running over his toned chest.

'You hungry? I brought home some lentil chilli from the café.'

'Sounds great. I can't remember having real

food since this investigation started.'

'Talking about which, how's it going?' I hesitated asking him, as I didn't want him to feel I was hounding him, or worse, interfering.

'It's the most complex investigation I've ever had. I'm glad CID are liaising with us so closely and we've been given extra manpower. I'm just frustrated that we've no forensics or witnesses to go on for any of the rapes.' Nick pushed his still-damp hair back from his forehead. We migrated to the kitchen and were waiting for the chilli heating in the microwave. I busied myself getting cutlery and bowls.

'Did Gill contact you? She said she would.'

'Yep. And we are concerned there could be a link but her attack was a while ago and not in this town so we've got to tread carefully. I've put a couple of our guys on this and some other similar historic rape cases that are now cold. It's more difficult when the victim is deceased and no one wants to talk, as in Chrissie Sims' case.'

'What if it's the same person? What if the uni failed to investigate and the same person has been getting away with this all these years?' I could feel the tension between us growing and I knew I was walking a thin line. Nick looked uncomfortable as I put his food down in front of him.

'Ally, that's exactly why we have got to tread carefully. If this is the same person and those responsible for protecting the public have failed to do that, the shit will hit the fan. I want to avoid any evidence being buried before we get a chance to find it. D' you understand?'

He was right and I nodded reluctantly. 'Are you still keeping an eye on Bill? He did go to that uni too.'

'Yes, and so did most of the seniors from this area. It'll take time. Anne has provided pretty strong alibis for him. And before you ask, we're still looking at Hargreaves too. Jake's looking at both of them as a priority. Hargreaves is interesting, though, because he moved back here just before the assaults started.'

'And he has priors,' I added.

'Jake also found out that his mother was in the same counselling group as the Carruthers girl.'

'Robyn? Really? That seems too much of a coincidence, but it's a small town, I guess, though it is a possible connection . . . if Simon is involved, that is.' Nick was right. This case was complicated. I just wished it would end. I sighed loudly as I got up to put my bowl in the sink.

'We'll get this guy, Ally,' he said, interpreting my sigh as a sign of my frustrating impatience. He stood up and put his arms around my waist from behind and kissed my neck.

'I hope so. Do you want seconds?' I picked up the bowl of left-over chilli.

'Hell, yeah,' he moaned into my ear, pushing the chilli bowl away and turning me around. I giggled as his kiss tickled my ear and I slid my hand into his boxers.

'My, oh my, detective. You really are ready for seconds, aren't you?'

***

Jinny

My hands were damp and clammy, clinging tightly to Charley's equally moist hand as we sat in the waiting room to see her brother. Nerves getting the better of us, I thought, but it wasn't helped by the over-heated, oppressive, stale air. The narrow hallway where we sat on old, rickety, wooden chairs, also served as a waiting area to the counselling rooms. Above her horn-rimmed glasses, from behind her makeshift desk in the far corner of the hall, Anne Bishopton glowered at our obvious gayness, making me want to challenge her. Charley could feel my rising irritation. She squeezed my hand tighter and gently shook her head to indicate that I should leave it, so I kept quiet for her sake. Charley was staring at the closed door, and I could see moisture in her eyes. She was emotional about this. Happy tears, she told me earlier before we got out the car. I could feel a lump in my throat, too. It had been years since I felt this happy.

The door opened and a couple I recognised from the café came out, hand in hand. They looked excited as they said goodbye to John Proctor. I guessed they were here for the same reason as us – to book their wedding – since they had both talked about nothing else for the last few weeks. I even knew what her dress looked like and what colour his tux would be – not grey, but grey with silver flecks through it. My heart skipped a beat as John noticed us sitting there. He walked towards us, his dark eyebrows drawn together questioningly.

'Charley, what're you doing here? You didn't say you were coming in.'

'I know, I probably should've booked in.' Charley jumped up, pulling me with her. 'But I wanted . . . *we* wanted to surprise you.'

Anne Bishopton snorted in disgust; about me and Charley's togetherness or arriving without an appointment, I didn't know. John seemed to consider it the latter.

'No need for appointments when it's family. That right, Anne?'

Anne hmphed as John ushered us in, shaking his head at Anne's rudeness.

'Take a seat. What brings you here?' John sat opposite us, his eyes briefly taking in our joined hands as he leaned in closer. His dark hair, which was greying slightly at the temples, was pushed back neatly and he wore simple black trousers and a dark blue shirt. He looked concerned as he waited patiently for Charley to explain our impromptu visit.

'John, I wanted you to be the first person I told, and to ask you something big.' Charley rushed on before John could answer. I would've done the same. I was nervous for her; family reactions are everything. While Ally had told us she was happy for us, I knew fine she'd have her doubts that it was too fast to get so attached. Especially marriage. But I kept that to myself. Ally would get used to us and I didn't want to upset Charley, who was ecstatic that Ally had already said how happy she was.

Charley's rushed speech interrupted my thoughts. '. . . So when can you fit us in?'

I tried not to laugh at John's look of surprise. 'I, erm . . .' He shook his head and took a deep breath.

Poor man, I felt sorry for him. He had no idea Charley was even seeing me, never mind ready to get married. I tried not to laugh, or giggle nervously, much as I wanted to.

'Charley, this is . . . is quite a turn of events. I'd no idea . . .' He waved his hand in my direction. 'How long've you been seeing each other?'

'A while. And we are sure about it before you ask,' Charley reassured him. 'To tell you the truth, when you asked me to come home, back to here, John, I really didn't want to come. Back to a place with dreadful memories.' John tried to interrupt, but Charley was on a roll. I was so proud of her. 'But you kept me busy at the refuge. And it was the right thing to do. I got counselling and then I met Jinny, at just

221

the right time.' John opened his mouth to speak again, but Charley rushed on regardless. 'And we've been together ever since. I feel that I can accept here as home now, John. Thanks to you, I love myself again, I love Jinny, and I love life.'

'Well. Well, Charley, I'm feeling a bit . . . a bit emotional.' John looked breathless, and to be honest I was too, since I'd been sitting there holding my breath at Charley's declarations.

'Just say you can fit us in soon? We don't want to wait.'

John shook his head as he rifled through a big register in front of him. His hands were shaking, running his finger down the pages of dates. I wanted to cry. This was more emotional than I'd thought. I was supposed to be here to support Charley, but she sat there smiling radiantly at me, all strong and confident.

'I can fit you in in three months' time. I've a cancellation the first Saturday of the month. We're booked solid till then with christenings, other weddings and the like.'

Charley jumped up and ran around the desk to hug him. He hugged her back. I could see his jaw clenching and there were tears in his eyes. He was obviously overwhelmed. Charley looked at me over his shoulder and I lost it. I rushed behind the desk to hug them both.

'We're getting married, we're getting married,' Charley chanted as she grabbed my hand and waved it around – just as Anne walked in with a tea tray and a face that would cause hell to freeze over.

CHAPTER SIXTEEN

Look at you lying there in a foetal position, drenched in sweat, rocking like a baby. Get a grip of yourself. You shake off the nightmare, but you can still feel the memories lingering like a filthy, black stain on a white sheet. You can still see your father's bloodshot eyes wide on his red face, pushed up against yours so close you smell decay on his breathe and feel droplets of his spit hit your cheek. You wanted to rub it off, but knew the movement would enrage him further. You curl up further in a protective ball, feeling every moment of the memory as if you were back there now. You whimper. You remember hearing his belt come off for punishment and you tense at the memory. You can still feel the sting like it had just happened. But you deserved it. He had to ensure that the sins of your biological mother would not stain you too.

You've always known what you were. Your parents have always told you where you came from. Your father tried to fix her too. To show her the right path, but she was too weak, broken. She couldn't be fixed, didn't want to be, so she ended her life with a rusty needle and a fatal dose of heroin after you were born. Your parents were there for you every day, unlike your broken mother.

Another memory flashes in. The bullies found you. You remember the humiliation. They pushed you around, spat on you, stripped you to your underwear and wrote faggot on your vest. The teachers were shocked when they found you tied to the chair in the storeroom. They called your parents. All your father could see was that word: faggot. Was that what you were? After all he had done to help you. But you convinced him eventually. He was proud you were not stained like your dead mother. This was the closest to him you ever felt. You're carrying on his work now. Fixing those that are broken. You know he'd be proud.

CHAPTER SEVENTEEN

Jinny

I unlocked the door and switched off the alarm, as Charley wrapped her arms around my waist from behind. I closed the door and turned to face her, to kiss her deep. I'd been dying to do that all evening at the coven but restrained myself. We'd only told those closest to us about our relationship. Others would find out in time.

'Let's get naked and try that spell right now.' Charley grinned up at me. I was only a couple of inches taller than her, but I loved that. I felt like her protector.

'I'm good with that,' I said as Charley started walking backwards into the kitchen, taking off her coat and dropping it, along with her scarf, and then her top. Seeing the cats sleeping peacefully in the kitchen corner, I followed her through to the warm living area. I stripped off too, and headed towards her, but Charley put up her hand to stop me moving.

'Uh uh. First the spell. You place the candles and I'll light them.' She bent over to roll up the rug – under which I'd painted a pentagram on the wooden floor – giving me a great arse view. I got the little jar candles from the bookcase and followed her around each point; as she placed each candle, I lit it, teasing her with my own bot when she looked.

'You got the doll?' I asked. I must admit I'd laughed my head off at first when Amira suggested making a voodoo doll, then I actually found it a bit creepy. I wasn't sure I wanted to use it, and had mentioned this to Charley on the way home, but Charley had it in her mind that it was harmless as long as it didn't have any human contents like hair, nails or blood; then she was okay with it.

'Yep, here.' She fished it out of her bag and held it up. It was just an old piece of hemp stuffed with cotton wool and tied at the neck and middle, but it still gave me the creeps. We also had a big hatpin – the coven had plenty of them – to stick in it.

We knelt in the middle of the pentagram, knees touching; candle, doll and pin in the centre. We held hands and together recanted the spell we had worked on tonight at the coven.

'Calling the universe to our need,
and spirits to protect us in our quest,
please hear the spell we screed,
to maketh the truth manifest.
Reveal the name of the rapist who
holds our town in ransom of fear.
End his reign of terror and strew.
Safety and protection far and near.'

At this point we both held the doll with one hand and with our other hands, mine over Charley's, we pushed the pin into the doll. Of course, at that exact point a cat yowled outside and we both jumped – and then laughed. We placed the doll back in the centre and continued our chant.

'Hear our call for the good of all

In our quest to manifest.'

We both lifted the candle that sat between us, and blew it out together.

'Now what?' I asked.

'Let's blow out the rest of the candles and put the rug back down and make the most of our nakedness. I'm horny as hell.'

'Not sure hell's the right sentiment.' I blew out each of the candles, lifting them and the doll to the bookshelf as Charley rolled the rug back out. By the time I'd finished, she was waiting, lying provocatively. 'I think I'm in heaven,' I said as I moved over her and met her lips.

***

Ally

I usually enjoyed attending professional development courses. They were a great way to catch up with old friends from uni and get positive, peer feedback on any difficult cases you had, but my heart just wasn't in it today. The course was after work so that counsellors didn't have to cancel any day time sessions and it was less formal than the regular class, but that didn't help me feel any less stressed. The half-hourly news reports requesting that anyone with any information regarding the rape cases to call the hotline, only made my nerves worse. I turned the volume down on the car radio, but it didn't help to quiet my mind as I drove the forty-five minute journey to the counselling suites. It would be late when I got back tonight, I thought, disheartened. At least it wasn't raining.

The counselling suites were housed in an upgraded, old sandstone building, which had been purchased by the university several years ago at the behest of the psychology and counselling department. They wanted somewhere purpose-built to train their postgraduate students and to facilitate the growing demand for talking therapies. The mature gardens and peaceful surroundings were the perfect backdrop for their needs. I parked in the street and walked up to the house so that I could stretch my legs and clear my mind before going in.

The course followed the usual format of introductions, agendas, lectures, and discussion time. During the breaks, I found myself sitting alone outside in the well-lit gardens with my packed sandwich instead of mingling with the others. I enjoyed the peace and quiet, the fresh, but cold air, as I tried to push the thoughts of the investigation, my clients and Nick and Jinny, as far out of my mind as possible.

Heading back inside, I stopped to look at the framed pictures of past graduate classes and counselling staff that had attended courses or worked at the suites. I found myself in one of the photographs and laughed at my curly hairstyle.

'We're a sight for sore eyes, aren't we, Ally?' I turned to see my old classmate, Carol, pointing at herself. She now taught part of the postgraduate course, working part-time to fit in with family life.

'Just a bit,' I replied. 'They were good times though, weren't they?' I thought how carefree life was back then, before the pressure of clients, before I saw how ugly and sad life could be for so many people.

We shuffled along the corridor pointing out all the old familiar faces and trying to remember their names.

'It's strange,' Carol said,. 'I walk past these pictures every day on my way to my office and even I forget who some of the people are. I guess that's life, isn't it? When things are so familiar you stop seeing them.' She looked at me, waiting for my response but my attention had been drawn to another picture. An old newspaper clipping, browned and ragged at the edges read: HERO HELPS CATCH SERIAL RAPIST. I moved closer to the article to get a better look at the picture under the headline.

'When was this?' I pointed to the article, my hand shaking as I held it out.

'Oh, it was, erm, about five years ago, I think. We had some nasty rapes around campus. Turned out it was a young guy, who had been working as the groundskeeper. They found out later he was on parole at the time for petty crime, but he was targeting young women who were students at the campus.'

'The groundskeeper?' I repeated, scanning the wording underneath the photograph. So many questions and doubts filled my mind.

'Yeah. We were so relieved he'd been caught. Thank God our hero sussed out who it was. It was such a bad time. Young women were petrified to walk the streets and campus. We didn't know who'd be next.' Carol shook her head as she remembered. 'Are you okay?'

'Eh . . . I . . . I need to make a call.' I was unable to pull my eyes away from the photograph. I pulled my phone out and mumbled to Carol that'd I'd catch her up in class.

Two notifications lit up my phone screen telling me I'd missed two calls and had two voicemails. I dialled the voicemail number and listened.

'Ally, it's Nick. Hope the course is okay? Just to let you know that Hargreaves has been let go. He was none too happy that Jinny reported him, so can you let her know to avoid any contact with him, and obviously call us if she sees him lurking about? Oh, and Jake was supposed to bring in Bishopton again to question him further about his daughter. According to her, Daddy was an abusive psycho and that's why she left, but it seems he's currently gone off radar. Jake hasn't checked in for a bit so I'll let you know if anything changes. Nothing is easy in this case. Miss you. See you tomorrow at some point . . . I hope.'

I loved it that things were progressing between us and that we'd grown to trust each other to talk about our jobs and the investigation, but I couldn't focus on any of that right now. I waited for the voicemail to move to the second message.

'Ally, it's me. Me and Charley spoke to John about us getting married. He was delighted and is gonna squeeze us in, in three months' time. Can you believe it? We're so excited. Anne Bishopton is a gay-hating bitch, though. Should've seen her face when we were waiting to see John. She definitely won't be getting an invitation. Anyway, I'll be at the coven tonight so probably catch up tomorrow. Speak soon, bye.'

I looked down the hall and watched everyone start to filter back to the class. Not me. I needed to contact Nick, and Jinny. I needed to warn them. I dialled Nick's number. No reply. Fuck. 'Nick, call me as soon as possible. Please,' I implored as I left the message. Jinny was the same.

Where the hell was everyone?

I left a message for her, too. I took one last look at the clipping as disbelief mingled with a rising, sickening feeling in the pit of my stomach.

How could this be?

I snapped a picture with my phone and ran out the door.

CHAPTER EIGHTEEN

The preparation for the intervention has been perfected over the years as you've cultivated your skill. It's always the same now. First, you go to your other place. A small cottage that sits at the bottom of a long lane. You bought it some time ago. No one knows it's yours. It's run down but cost very little. It has all the basics. You don't need much, and it's a place where you keep your kit and plan your moves without any interference.

You're ready to begin now. You push the button on your old CD player and the notes from a melancholic and sombre opera fill the air as you begin your process. You clean the shower room with strong bleach, and like a practiced surgeon using an aesthetic technique, open a new scrubbing brush, razor and overalls. It's as close to a sterile process as you can get. You shower with detergent that reddens your skin, but has the benefit of removing oils and scents. Then you shave. The blade scrapes over your skin, removing every hair on your body apart from your head. Your hair is cut close, so you scrub and comb your hair and scalp just to be sure, but your head will be covered nonetheless. Then the brush. It scratches over your body removing dead and loose cells. No trace will be left. The process is your own metamorphosis. Like a snake shedding its skin to grow, or a caterpillar transforming. Both you and your chosen one will be doing the same. Growth and rebirth.

A new paper towel dries your body. Your skin is red, tight and taut. It stings, reminding you of how your skin felt after your father used his belt – a reminder of how important your work is. His punishment fixed you, just as you fix them. You pull the black overalls on over your naked body. A double zipper top and bottom, which make it easy to get your dick out when the time is right. You place small packs of sterile gloves and condoms in the zipped pocket. A tight balaclava, rolled up, not over your face, for now, secures your hair. You stand in front of the mirror as you go over the details of the intervention in your mind. You hadn't expected to be working this soon after your last one. But things changed unexpectedly. She's responsible for this, and your plan had to be drawn up hastily, so you've had to replay it many times, checking for potential errors. This one is all about tying up loose ends. Loose ends that you hadn't expected. But you'll fix them. Fix them for good this time.

CHAPTER NINETEEN

Jinny

Charley and I moved to the bedroom after we'd satiated ourselves with each other, with food, and had checked mummy cat was also fed and content. I finished brushing my teeth, put on my PJs and joined Charley in bed. We laughed at our nightwear: my T-shirt said 'hers' on it and Charley's vest said the same. Ally bought them for us after we told her we were getting married. Charley thought it was sweet of her, but I knew Ally still had her doubts about us tying the knot so soon and that this was her way of appeasing any guilt she had of not being one hundred percent supportive.

'What're you reading?' I asked, looking at the tattered hardback A4 sized volume she was leafing through.

'Come and see. It's John's yearbook. I must've taken it, thinking it was mine.'

'Yearbook?' I asked, wondering why she brought it with her.

'Yeah, you wanted to see pics of me growing up, my past . . . remember?'

'Oh yeah. I said I'd look out mine, too. Sorry, I completely forgot. So if that's John's yearbook there won't be any photos of you, will there?' I looked disappointedly over her shoulder while she flicked through the pages. 'Wait – stop. Is that Bill?' I saw a group photo of some younger and older kids laughing and fooling around.

'I think it is. Let me check the names. Yep, third left, William Bishopton.'

We looked at the picture in disbelief. There was Bill with an arm-lock on an older girl's neck. Everyone else was laughing but the girl didn't look too happy about it.

'Who's the girl?' I asked, pulling half the book towards me so I could get a better look. I read the caption: FORMER SCHOOL PUPILS, NOW AT UNIVERSITY, HELP COACH THE NETBALL AND FOOTBALL TEAMS.

'Fuck,' we both exclaimed at the same time. 'Gill Garby.'

'Look, that's John on her other side. That's his uncomfortable-but-going-along-with-it face.' Jinny pulled the book back, scanning for any more similar photos. 'Being bigger in build, Bill gave everyone a hard time, John said.'

'That's awful. It's the strangle hold that freaks me out.'

'Yeah, I know. Too close to the bone, if you ask me.'

'Hey, look. That's Jake De Stefano too, a coach for the football team it says. He hasn't changed much.'

'So it is. I remember all the girls in my year swooning after him, and all the uni student coaches.'

'Christ, Charley, do you think this is the reveal spell? Do you think it's giving us a clue? Revealing Bill?'

'Oh my God. Shit. Yeah. I'll take it to Nick in the

morning. See what he thinks.' Charley put the yearbook on the floor and kissed me goodnight as I leant over to turn off the bedside light.

I had no sooner done that when we heard a noise outside, a cat yowl and the patio light came on. Then another cat yowl, its cry louder than before.

'Jeez, I hope that's not another lost cat, or worse, a male cat wanting his way with our cat.' I swung my legs over the edge of the bed as more yowls rang out. 'I was gonna ignore it, but . . .' More cries. 'Okay, dammit. I'll check.'

'It's pitch dark out. Do you want me to come too?' Charley was looking nervously at me and probably hoping the noise would just stop.

'No, it's fine. I'll scream if I'm in trouble.'

'Now you're scaring me. Give me a minute to pee and then I'm coming too.'

***

Ally

'Shiiit. Why isn't anyone answering?' I screamed at my phone as I threw it onto the passenger seat of my car and banged my fists off the steering wheel. I'd pulled into the service station to refuel and tried calling Nick and Jinny again but just got voicemails instead. I'd already left messages so there was no point leaving more. As the phone hit the seat a notification rang out. A missed call and another message. I realised that someone had been trying to reach me as I was calling out. It was Nick.

'Ally, just to give you a heads up. Jake hasn't checked in yet so it's safe to presume Bill's still off radar. I've checked with Anne, but she has no clue where he is. I know you'll be worried and seeing as

235

you're out of town and won't have had a chance to tell Jinny about Hargreaves I'll head over to Jinny's to check on her and Charley. Sorry for all the messages.'

Frustrated that I kept missing calls yet relieved that Nick would be checking on Charley and Jinny, I started the engine again, but heading back onto the motorway I just couldn't shake the bad feeling I had – and I still had a half hour's drive to get back.

CHAPTER TWENTY

You've been watching them. Watching them come home. Watching them fuck on the floor like animals. Watching them insert plastic objects into each other. They're fucking filthy sluts and you will fix them. You'll remove their shame in the same way your father removed your biological mother's shame. It's a two for one deal. You'll fix them both . . . for good.

The stray cat in your arms cries loudly in pain as you twist its ear. How fortunate for you that it chose now to meander through the slut's garden. You twist its ear again and it cries and squirms to escape. A light upstairs goes on and you pull the balaclava down over your face. You reach into your kit and remove two hoods. This fix will be the perfect culmination to your work in this town. Inside your overalls, you feel your cock harden in anticipation. You're ready. Time to tie up loose ends.

CHAPTER TWENTY-ONE

Jinny

I couldn't wait for Charley to have her pee; that cat was in trouble. Its cries were tearing at my heart. I shoved on my wellies, grabbed my coat from the hook and pulled it on. The cat howled again. I flung open the door to see where the noise was coming from. A tortoiseshell cat lay motionless under the tree. Poor thing, had it fallen? Was I too late? I ran to it, my bare knees sinking into the cold, wet grass as my hands felt its warm body. Was it breathing? As I bent over to see if it was alive, something covered my head and quickly tightened on my neck. I couldn't understand what was happening. Was Charley playing some sort of joke? 'Ch– Charl . . .' I tried to speak, and my hands went up wanting to get it off, but it was getting tighter and tighter: pressure on my neck, pain in my eyes, my nose, the veins in my face bulging.

Can't breathe. Help. Please. I was screaming in my head, my voice unheard. I tried to get up but was pulled back. Dizzy, buzzing, Charley, I yelled in my head, but there was only blackness.

I was floating, dreaming. I could hear someone crying, begging someone else not to do it. Not do what? Was it Charley? It was. It was Charley. I was having a nightmare about Charley, except it felt real. I was cold. Between my legs felt cold and wet. And then it came back to me. I had been attacked, choked. I must have fainted. Was it the rapist? I tried to breathe deeply to stop myself from losing consciousness again. Bile rose at the back of my throat. I felt sick. Had I been raped? Was he now attacking Charley? Oh my God. My hands were numb and anchored to something. It was my ankles. My wrists were tightly bound to my ankles with duct tape and I was lying on my side on the cold damp grass.

They sure didn't tell you how to get out of this kind of bondage at self-defence.

Damn. Trying to inhale deeply, I could smell the wet earth. My heart raced as the dizziness subsided, and the buzzing lessened as I filled my lungs with the cold night air. My eyes were open and it was still dark, and I still had something over my head and Charley was still crying hysterically. I had to get my bearings.

'Why? Why a' you doing this t'us? Who a' you? Take off tha' hood so I can see, y' coward. Anshwer me. Who a' you?' I slurred, hoping to distract him from Charley. From what I could tell she was probably tied up and hooded outside too. Although I felt wet down below, my shorts were still on. I could smell urine; I'd peed myself. I hadn't been raped – yet. I didn't think so, at least.

Please, don't let him have raped Charley.

'Ah, you are both awake now.' His voice was low, barely audible.

Why was he whispering? Was it so we wouldn't

know who he was? I couldn't make out the voice, but there was something familiar about it. Damn. I could overpower him, I was sure, if I wasn't tied up. Fuck, fuck, fuck.

'Wha' the fuck d'you wan'? The puleesh a' on 'e way,' I bluffed. 'Y' think 'd come 'shide alone a' night 'thout phonin' 'em, knowin' 'ere's a rapisht abou'?'

He laughed at my pathetic attempts to scare him. 'Yes, you did,' he threw back. 'I've been watching you. Maybe you should've closed your blinds. I've seen the obscenities you get up to. You disgust me with your perversions. I've tried to help. Don't you remember, Charley? Have you forgotten your lesson so quickly?'

Charley, who had been sobbing quietly up to that point, went quiet.

'Ah, you do remember. But not well enough to stop falling back to your abhorrent ways. Well, don't worry, my dear. This time the fix will be permanent.'

I panicked. What did he mean? Was he going to rape her again? The adrenaline surge cleared my head, sobered me up quickly. I was frightened to make a noise and lose my only sense, my only way of knowing where he was and what was happening. But I had to say something.

'Leave 'er alone y' fucker. Don't fucking go near 'er. I'll bloody kill you. I'll kill–'

'Enough,' I heard him snap near me.

I whipped myself into a sitting position hoping to hit him with my head. But nothing.

'Don't worry. I'm saving her till last. I'll be starting with you,' his voice went on. 'You will get your penance while Charley watches. I'm going to remove her temptation once and for all.'

My heart raced and I felt sick, just imagining what he had planned. I couldn't see. Charley was whimpering so quietly I could just make her out. Small whimpers that told me she was petrified. He was still uttering his macabre plan, moving further and further away. 'Then Charley, your final punishment. There seems to be no fixing you. So we will make it permanent this time. I will enjoy that. Sending you off, penance paid.'

I heard Charley inhale. I felt even sicker. What was the bastard up to? I kept quiet so I could hear what was happening. Maybe I could take a chance and throw myself towards his voice. Would he see me coming and kill me?

What was he doing? Who the fuck was he?

I was immobilised by the unknown, by being blind.

'Open your eyes, Charley. Now you can watch, Charley. See her be transformed by what is right, what is meant to be. See her leave this world, her sins forgiven. Don't worry. You'll not be far behind her.'

I was so distracted by what he was saying that I only realised he was nearer me when it was too late. My head hit the grass as he pulled my ankles forward. I fought against the dizziness and nausea. He was fumbling with my clothes. I could feel him look for the waistband of my shorts. I tried to twist away but he pushed me back.

'You only make it more painful if you struggle,' he warned.

'Go fuck y' shelf,' I roared, rolling side to side, hoping I could knock him over, but he was too sturdy. He grabbed my coat at the neck, pulling me forwards and then thumping me back down. My head was spinning. Then he did it again. I was close to losing consciousness; the buzzing was back, roaring louder in my ears . . . louder and louder and then I heard screaming . . . louder and louder.

At first, I thought it was me. He was back at my waistband, tugging, tugging, but then the screams stopped and a weight toppled him onto me, knocking me onto my side. My hood came half off. I could see the grass. I rolled onto my back away from him, to get out from under him, and I kept rolling, onto my front, my face in the grass. The hood fell off as I shifted my weight back to fall onto my shins. I could hear Charley behind me.

'Charley, y' okay? Charley?' I twisted round. Charley was standing looking down at him. His back was towards me, his balaclava in Charley's taped hands in front of her. One of her ankles still had tape stuck to it but she'd managed to get free to get him off me. I used my knees to walk round to face them. Charley was staring open-mouthed and he was shaking. No he wasn't shaking, he was laughing. *Laughing.* What the fuck?

'Charley, God dammit, Charley run and get help,' I shouted. She didn't move. He stood up; she still didn't move. 'Charley, for fuck's sake, get out of here.'

He moved towards her. This time she backed away, her facial expression still in shock. I had no idea who she was looking at. It could've been anybody with the kit he was wearing, his hair greased flat. The hair was dark, that's all I could make out. Was it Bill Bishopton? It could be anyone with dark hair. My heart was pounding in my head. I couldn't move, trussed up like a Christmas turkey. And Charley was mesmerised. As she backed off, he kept walking towards her.

'Help!' I shouted, knowing the chances of anyone hearing would be minimal out here, amongst the closed shops and empty roads. My eyes never left Charley as she was backed right against the wall. He moved up to her and touched her face. I saw he had blue nitrile gloves on. Charley's eyes were filled with tears. 'Please Charley, do something,' I beseeched. His hand slid to her breast beneath the heavy jumper she'd pulled on. She didn't move. Tears rolled down her face.

Who was it was paralysing Charley like this?

Maybe it was just her fear of being raped again. Maybe she thought *she'd* save *me* by distracting him. Dammit.

'Leave her alone. Come on, rape me, y' filthy bastard. I've never had a man. I bet you'd love that. Y' like virgins, don't you? I know about you. Raping young innocent women. Well, come and get me.'

Slowly, he turned towards me. And now I knew why Charley was too crippled to retaliate.

The Reverend John Proctor, Charley's brother, looked back at me while he fondled her breast. *Baaaaaastaaaaaard*.

No wonder Charley had shut down. I felt the energy leave my own legs, the nausea rise in my throat again, and I felt powerless as I watched him take a knife from his pocket and flick it open.

'Ah, Jinny, maybe I'll let you watch me with Charley first. Enjoy the show. Don't worry, I won't kill her yet. I want her to see what I'll do to you.'

'Wh . . . wh . . . why? Why would you do this?'

'Don't you get it? It's wrong. You are an abomination. God knows it, my father knew it, and you know it too. Deep down, you all know it. It usually just takes one fix to show you all the right way. It worked with Charley till you poisoned her with your perversions. You've ruined her, you know. You're to blame for this.'

He ran his knife over Charley's jumper, as far as her neck. He pushed the blade into her skin, drawing

243

a point of blood. Charley never flinched; her eyes were staring into space. He tucked the knife into the neck of her jumper and drew it all the way down, slicing it open, along with her pyjama top. Using his left hand to lift the garments away, he caressed her breast while his right held the knife to her throat.

'But she's your sister. You're fucking sick, John. You need help.'

'Ah, but she's *not* my sister, Jinny. *She* doesn't even know that. Oh no. Father adopted her when he realised her mother was dying of cancer and was going to give Charley up to her lesbian aunt. Her mother was a good friend of the family. She was worried about her daughter getting perverted. My father gave her mother money to have the best of care at the end of her life and his promise to look after her daughter in a *normal* family. She was a good, God-fearing woman and saw the truth in that. But Charley here was tainted. Going away to college, being led astray by wanton whores.' He shook his head. 'Not only did she come back and parade her deviances to my parents, she *killed* them with her poisonous confession. I taught her the truth of the Lord. I had cured her and counselled her. I had fixed her till you came along. *You* undid all of that. And I never even saw it coming.'

'But y' profess to support gays, y' counsel people coming out.' Jinny was reeling with anger. 'You have a women's shelter, for fuck's sake. How?' Jinny shook her head trying to get clarity. 'Why?'

'That's the easy part. All of that helps me guide them to see the error of their ways. If that doesn't work, their names go on my waiting list for a fix. Do you know how many women I've managed to save? Do you? Twenty-three so far.'

'Saved? You killed Karen Whitelaw. And her

innocent baby. You fuckin' murdered them in cold blood.'

'No, that was an accident. Stupid bitch hadn't charged her phone. She wasn't meant to die.'

'You killed an innocent baby.'

'No, I helped that baby. Don't you see that? It would've grown up in sin, surrounded by the perversions of its parents. I prevented that. It wouldn't ever have to suffer. It didn't have a good family to save it. I was lucky. My father saved me.'

'What do you mean?' Jinny tried to understand what John was implying. 'Your mother was a lesbian?'

'No, no. *My* mother was a God-fearing woman. Her *sister* was the lesbian, she was *sick*. *My* poor mother couldn't have children. She took her *perverted* sister in to help her change her ways. Help her kick her drug habit, help her see the evil in her homosexuality. But no, she left that sanctuary and shacked up with another female drug addict. My mother was distraught. My father was a well-respected judge. He couldn't have this shame brought to his door. They took her back. My father showed her what *real* love was. *I* was born from that.'

This monster's thinking revolted Jinny; his hatred for lesbians was psychotic. 'Your *real* mother was a lesbian? Are you saying your father raped her like *you* raped all these other women?' It was making sense now, his warped thinking.

'You don't see it. You can't. You're an abomination. Just like my biological mother. My father tried so hard to teach her what was right. But she didn't learn. She left again. Went right back to that slut and overdosed.'

He was insane. Jinny was terrified for Charley as she watched his hand fondle her breast. 'You're so fuckin' warped. You sick bas–'

245

'*I* was the lucky one. I had a *real* mother and father who kept me on the path to righteousness. And it's *my* duty now to help others.' He moved his left hand from Charley's breast into her shorts, between her legs. 'I'm going to really enjoy this, even more than the others. This is your retribution, Charley.' His lips moved to her neck as he spoke, licking her neck.

Charley hadn't moved. Her eyes remained glazed over and her mouth dribbled saliva down her chin. I didn't know what to do to get him away from Charley. My legs and hands were numb with being tied, the cold, and my position. I couldn't move either. I was as powerless as Charley.

'You're a sick, sick bastard, John, and they will find you. You'll pay for this. See the camera above the door? Recording all of this. You've been caught, John. That film goes directly to an online server. You can't destroy that evidence. Get out of here while you can.' I lied. The camera only went to my computer, but he wouldn't know that, and if anything happened to me, at least the evidence would be there.

His hand stopped moving and he turned to face me. 'I know where the camera is and I'm not in line to be seen. When I was, my face was covered. So I have no fear.' He removed his hand from Charley's shorts and unzipped the fly from the bottom of his overalls. His dick sprung out. He took a condom from his pocket and ripped it open with his teeth. He sheathed himself and put the wrapper back in his pocket. I noticed how careful he was being to not leave evidence. He turned his attention to Charley's shorts and started to pull down one side. 'Enjoy the show, Jinny . . . You're next . . .'

'Charley. Please, Charley,' I cried, struggling against my restraints, begging Charley to snap out of it. 'Call on your inner Goddess . . .'

John sneered at my fruitless pleas. She was like a puppet in his hands as he scraped his knife over her skin above her shorts. Then I noticed a spark. Just a small glimmer of strength as Charley's eyes refocused on me – and her body stiffened. It happened so fast; all I could do was watch. She shoved all her body weight onto him, shoving from her shoulder as she pushed him forward away from her as she fell to the ground. He was caught off guard. His foot caught a loose cobble in the patio and he lost his balance, stumbling backwards into the sharp point of the broken tree branch I'd snapped in my cat-rescuing deed. I watched shock register on his face as he realised he was impaled. He tried to pull himself off but before he did Charley was pushing up from the ground, her face full of hate and anger.

'Charley. Charley.' It was John's turn to plead as she raised her bound hands and, with a determined yell, shoved him further onto the branch.

John screamed and pleaded for her to stop, but this Charley was looking for closure. There was no stopping her now. This was my Charley. She punched, kicked and punched, till John stopped screaming, the blood pouring from the branch where it had broken through his overalls, and foaming from his mouth, the tears still streaming from his eyes. His open, dead eyes.

'Go fuck yourself, you lying bastard,' Charley spat and ran over to me. She fell to her knees in front of me, looped her arms round my neck and pulled us cheek to cheek, hugging me tight.

'Charley,' I cried, our tears mingling.

'I . . . I . . . killed him. I killed him, Jinny–' She broke off, hugging me tighter.

'Look at me, Charley, look at me.' I pulled back to look into her eyes. 'You had no choice. He was going to kill us both. You heard him. And after us, there'd be no stopping him. He'd have gone on killing.'

'I know. I know. You're right. We'd have died tonight, wouldn't we?'

'No doubt, Charl. None whatsoever.'

'Will . . . will I go to prison?'

'No. God, no,' I reassured her, but inside I didn't really know. 'It was self-defence. He fell back right onto that branch. He fell back so hard when you pushed him away. It was accidental.'

'Yeah?'

'Fuck, yeah.'

A car squealed to a halt outside and there was a sudden banging at the gate. Under the force, the wooden gate burst, and Ally tumbled through. For a moment, she stood staring at the scene, then she looked at Charley and me.

'Oh my God, what the hell–' She ran straight to us and grabbed us both in a hug. 'Oh God, I knew something was wrong. I just knew it.' She pulled back and ripped at the duct tape binding both Charley and me. 'Are you alright? What happened?'

'We're not hurt,' I reassured her. 'Not physically.' I wondered if Charley was emotionally and mentally okay after all that. He did actually abuse her again.

Charley looked at me and kissed me on the lips. 'I'm fine. The bastard's dead. He can't hurt me anymore in any way. I'm free of him.'

Ally looked at me. I knew she was wondering if Charley was really okay. I knew she was. I nodded.

'Oh God, I was so scared. I knew it was him. I knew it. I couldn't get you on the phone, God, I thought he'd killed you both,' Ally cried over us. 'What happened?' she asked again, helping us both up off the cold ground.

I said quickly, 'He fell onto that branch–'

But Charley cut me off. 'I pushed him, Ally,' she admitted.

'Well, it isn't your fault he fell right onto the branch, Charley,' Ally reassured her.

'Yeah, but I kept pushing . . . I wanted . . . I wanted to . . .'

I looked at my sister. I could see she realised what Charley was asking. She was asking Ally for forgiveness, for her to rationalise her actions as a professional, to bring her into our circle of trust. I relaxed. I knew my sister.

At that point another car screeched to a halt and Nick ran in. He, too, surveyed the scene. He stared at John's limp body hanging on the tree, then turned to us, Ally standing with me and Charley each side of her, her arms around our waist to support us.

'What the fuck–'

'He fell.' All three of us spoke in unison.

CHAPTER TWENTY-TWO

Unlike normal Monday lunchtimes, the café was crowded. Jinny observed a feeling of quiet relief now the rapist was dead. And lots of people wanted to thank Charley for making it happen. Who could blame them, Jinny mused, staring at Charley who was having to reassure Ally for the hundredth time that she was fine and didn't need counselling.

'I'm telling you, Ally, it's like a heavy burden has been lifted and it's all so clear to me now. I always had a feeling John didn't like me, and my parents seemed distant. I mean, my father was always strict and I was terrified of him, and my mother worshipped the ground he walked on, so never really gave us much attention. And I did wonder why John seemed to be the golden boy, but I always thought that was because he was the first-born son. I had no idea at all that I was adopted. John really was sick.'

'I always knew you had a strength in you, Charley. You'd repressed so much, it changed your identity,' Ally admitted, patting Charley's hand. 'Are you going to see if you can find your aunt?'

'Jinny and I have found her already!' Charley

beamed. 'She's got two daughters, one older than me and one younger, and she can't wait to meet me.'

'She's invited us over next weekend to stay with her,' Jinny added. 'Nice house near the Devon coast. And she said to come stay with her for a while after the wedding.'

'Oh, Charley, that's amazing news.' Ally looked at Jinny. 'I'm glad the wedding's still on, I really and truly am happy for you both. What you two have been through . . .' Ally shook her head, swallowing. 'You two are so meant to be.' Ally cuddled Jinny beside her, and then leaned over the table to cuddle Charley.

'Hey, Ally?' Jinny tugged at her sister's sleeve. 'Here's Nick.'

Ally waved him over to their table, squeezing Jinny's hand under the table. Jinny knew that now Ally genuinely was happy about her relationship. And Jinny recognised that Ally was well-smitten by Nick. Jinny squeezed back, happy for her.

'Hey,' Nick said, taking in everyone as he sat in the empty space beside Charley.

'How's it winding up at the station?' Ally asked.

'Are you sure you want to discuss this? You know . . .' Nick was implying that it may be too fragile for Charley to hear, Jinny surmised, but everybody was more than keen to hear and told him so.

'The team has worked hard on this. We found papers in Proctor's office that led us to a house he bought some years ago. It was out in the sticks so a good place for him to prepare for his crimes and get rid of evidence. We found a brazier in the garden where he'd burnt used overalls and other stuff. And, Ally, you were right about him refining his behaviour.'

'How?'

'Well, his journal–'

'He had a journal?' Charley asked.

'Yeah, we found that and some newspaper clippings of the rapes. In it he said he'd been using the crematorium to dispose of his evidence at other places, but was nearly caught. Says he decided to find the isolated house so that would never happen again. He kept his supplies there, too. At the back of the journal he had a list of names.'

'Names?' Ally asked.

'Yeah,' Nick continued. 'We traced all the towns he preached in and compared the names in his book to the reported rapes. We've found the majority of them. A few have died or committed suicide and a few are untraceable.' Nick surveyed the table.

'That was the list he talked about,' Charley said, looking at Jinny.

Jinny realised her mouth was open and she was as gobsmacked as everyone else. 'Please, continue,' she said. 'What'll happen to his victims?'

'Nothing. We don't want to upset people that have already come to terms with what happened to them. But the men he framed for the crimes will be released and compensated. There's going to be a news documentary about it, so any of his victims that didn't get closure or didn't have a perpetrator to blame will be able to contact the hotline set up for help or counselling.' Nick looked at Ally.

'You're doing the counselling, aren't you?' Jinny asked.

'Nick's asked me to be on the team of counsellors,' Ally admitted.

'Head the team,' Nick corrected.

Ally nodded. 'I think I can help, given I've been so close to the cases here.'

'You'd be ideal,' Charley confirmed. 'You certainly helped me. I'm pretty sure John's

252

counselling would've subtly eroded me. It's strange how I never saw it at the time. And all those women . . .'

'Was Gill's friend from school and uni, Chrissie, on the list?' Ally asked.

'She was his first.' Nick confirmed. 'Dates and times he listed match too. There was another name there that was scored off. It was the only one in his journal he seemed to have a change of mind about.'

'Can you tell us who?' Ally asked. 'Do we know them?'

Nick looked at Jinny and nodded slowly. 'It was Fiona Rudd.'

'What the f–' Jinny exploded.

'She was your ex, wasn't she?' Nick looked over at Ally. 'Ally had mentioned it.'

'Yeah. Oh hell, was this my fault? Was it because I mentioned to John I'd had a break up – that time I went and did the workshop?' Jinny looked at Charley. 'When was it, Nick?'

'Just before he raped Denise.'

'That's about the right time. Christ, she could've been raped because of me.'

'Or because of me,' Charley piped up. 'John asked me about you and your break up after you'd gone. I thought he was just being concerned. He even told me to remind you he was there if you wanted to talk about it.'

Ally reached out and patted Charley and Jinny's joined hands across the table.

'Neither of you could've known. So neither of you has anything to feel guilty about. And anyway, he didn't touch her.' Ally looked to Nick. 'Any idea why?'

'Just said in his journal, 'already been fixed'.'

Jinny held up her phone open at Fiona's social feeds: photos of Fiona and Kevin looking cosy. 'Guess this is why. Seems she's still with Kev. I'm glad.' Jinny sighed in relief.

'Wait,' Charley interrupted. 'So he was going to rape 'out of town'', she used her fingers to quote, 'Fiona, and then because he didn't need to 'fix' her, he moved on to 'out of town' Denise?'

'Seems so. Why?' Nick asked, clearly not seeing a connection.

'You guys,' Ally chided. 'I'm sure it was just coincidence and not any hoky poky spells.'

'What are you talking about?' Nick asked.

'Nothing,' Ally, Jinny and Charley replied in unison.

Nick looked at them, raised his brows, and took a deep breath. 'You've no idea how good he was,' he admitted. 'The list and journal give us a timeline. It shows clearly how he's escalated and refined his MO. He became more sadistic as he progressed.'

'I'm sure forensic psychologists will be all over it,' Ally was trying to find a thread of value in his evil deeds.

'He also journaled about who he was setting up to frame. He would frame someone to take the fall and then moved on somewhere else,' Nick continued.

'I guess that's why he was never caught. Especially as he'd refined his MO along the way, authorities never pieced together it was same person. He was so close to getting away with it again,' Ally said.

'Yeah, he came so near to framing Bill, too,' Jinny pointed out.

'He used Anne to find out when Bill was home with her so she would be a weak alibi. He had a calendar of their itinerary. Even on the night of your attack Bill didn't have an alibi for that specific time.'

'If it hadn't been for Charley's bravery and Ally

realising the attacker was John, Bill would be in prison and we'd be dead,' Jinny added.

'God, don't say that,' Ally said. 'He was so calculated. I was shocked when I saw the clipping of him. It was then I realised he knew Gill from school, too, and he had access to everyone who was raped here. He was the common denominator. It all came together in a flash and I knew you two were next. God, I was frantic, when no one answered their phones. Bloody frantic. Thank God, I got Nick at last, who'd been coming to warn you about sleazy Simon.'

Jinny laughed. 'Least of my worries. I can well handle sleazy Simon.'

'You won't need to,' Nick said. 'The whole family are moving. Again. They hate scandal. And Simon is scandal to them. Just the fact that we brought him in for questioning has got them running in shame.'

'Well, good riddance. The gym was tense if he was there,' Jinny confessed. 'I even started following him about after that incident with the girl. He didn't like being stalked. He left if he saw me.'

'Yeah, he reported you to us when we had him in. But made it out more like he was threatening you. I guess he was the one feeling threatened.'

'What happened to Bill?' Ally asked. 'You said he'd went AWOL.'

Nick laughed. 'Anne told Jake he'd gone off on a bender to Cambridge. So Jake got a list of all his old haunts from when he lived there, hence why Jake couldn't be found. But . . . Well, you are not going to believe me, but you'll see for yourself soon enough. Bill turned up at the station the next morning pleading to be told where his daughter was. He'd gone off on a drinking binge in his garden shed, drinking his home-made wine. Realised his life had turned to shit since he'd adopted his homophobic stance. Said he'd begged God for a sign. Next thing he gets a text from Anne to say the police were looking for him, and their daughter was at the station. He took that as a sign from the big man himself. And now he's, wait for it . . .' Nick hesitated.

Jinny hated the suspense. She'd no idea what was coming next. 'What?' she pushed. 'Tell us.'

Nick pulled a newspaper out his pocket, opened it at a page of adverts, and planted it on the table.

'What the fuck?' Jinny squealed.

'Well, I guess we could always have our reception there.' Charley laughed.

'*Not!*' Jinny laughed, staring at the advert for the hotel, which was welcoming wedding receptions for all genders. The advert was part of a larger story about Bill and Micky, his daughter, getting reunited. Bill publicly apologised to the community for his past behaviour. Jinny laughed again. 'What a bloody turnaround.'

'Yeah,' Nick agreed. 'His daughter and her partner are staying there at the moment and helping with modernising the place now.'

'I guess Anne's had a change of heart, too?' Charley asked. 'The looks she gave us when we went to John to book our wedding would have frozen hell over.'

'Anne's in her element,' Ally put in. 'Been to see me to tell me she doesn't need counselling but wanted me to know Bill's a new man. Having her daughter back meant everything. It was nice to see.'

'Right,' Nick stood up to put his coat on. 'I'd better get back to work. See you later, Ally?'

'Yeah. I'll see you at the cottage. You've got your key?'

'Of course,' Nick replied casually, showing off a shiny new key attached to his keyring.

'Woo-hoo,' Jinny and Charley hooted together.

'Behave,' Ally scolded, slapping Jinny on the shoulder.

Nick said his goodbyes and quickly pecked Ally on the cheek as he passed her seat.

'Going well then?' Jinny asked when he'd left.

'It is. I'm saying no more. Anyone want more coffee, tea?'

'Yeah, get me a matcha,' Jinny said.

'Lemon ginger tea for me please,' Charley added. 'And a bit of lemon drizzle cake too, please.'

'Be right back,' Ally said and headed to the counter. She returned and placed a tray in the middle of the table. Everyone helped themselves to their order.

'I just want to say,' Jinny said between mouthfuls of tea, 'the spell we did that night, the reveal spell, well, I guess it really worked.'

'Oh, please, don't start back on that again,' Ally begged. 'If you want to believe that, well, that's up to you. Just leave me out of it.'

Charley looked at Jinny and smiled before joining in. 'But, Ally, how can you deny after all that, that the spell didn't work? The yearbook had his photo in it. And all the other spells worked too, in some way.'

'Bollocks! We agreed Simon rigged it and there was no spell. The rest were coincidence; the yearbook had just about half the town in it. You two are reading too much into something that isn't there, just to make it fit your theory.'

'Sis, look at the amount of times we got results. No way was it a coincidence.'

'There's no way you will convince me

otherwise. You two can carry on with the coven or your little witchy spells, but after what happened the last time I'd have thought you'd want to leave that well alone.'

'I suppose,' Jinny admitted. 'That was scary as fuck. I know it was just a set of circumstances coming together, *but* it was too much of a coincidence for me for the spell to bring him to our door that very night.'

'Yeah, don't worry Ally,' Charley butted in. 'I think we're off the spells for a while. That was too close for comfort. Literally. I think we'll skip dabbling with spells, and the coven, for the foreseeable.'

'Good. I really don't want to be worrying about you two getting into any more trouble.' Ally finished her coffee and pulled on her jacket. 'Oh, what did the vet say about the cat?'

'He was fine,' Jinny said, smiling. 'A few ear and neck bruises and a burst blood vessel in one eye due to being nearly strangled, but he's all fine now.'

'Oh, thank God,' Ally sighed. 'He was so limp I thought he was a goner.'

'Vet said he was in shock, most likely. But his owner has him home again and is keeping him indoors for a couple of weeks to make sure he's fully recovered.'

'I'd better bloody well get back to work.' Ally looked at her watch. As she stood to leave both her and Jinny's phone rang out with a loud notification.

Jinny laughed as she unlocked hers. 'Looks like we hit that target on the holiday fund, thanks to the swear app. Or maybe I should say wedding fund?'

'Wedding fund?' Charley asked Jinny.

'Yeah, we've got enough money in the swear app account to pay for us three to go to somewhere warm and sunny for the wedding.'

'But–' Charley started.

258

Jinny held her hand up. 'Ally and I have already agreed,' she said.

'We have.' Ally reassured her. 'I need a break after all this. It'll be good to get a holiday. Maybe even have some company on it, if Nick can get the time off?'

'You and Nick can be our witnesses. Ooh, I'm excited now.' Charley beamed.

'Anyway, on that positive note, I'm off.' As Ally left the café, she looked back to watch her sister and Charley through the window, and she smiled. They looked as thick as thieves, she thought warmly. She took a deep breath and filled her lungs with air. It was a chilly, but crisp, sunny day. Today felt fresh and new. For the first time in a while Ally was optimistic. Her relationship with Nick was growing and her career was moving in a new direction. Things felt good, she reflected, as she crossed the road and headed to the centre.

EPILOGUE

Jinny

Glancing down at the newspaper Nick had left on the table, I held my breath to stop myself from swearing out loud.

'What's up?' Charley asked, waving to Ally through the café window and then turning back to me.

I turned the paper to face her. Its front page displayed a large headline and a picture of some angry-looking mothers, waving some placards.

She looked at it and then looked to me. Then she looked at the heading again. LOCALS OBJECT TO REGISTERED SEX OFFENDER MOVING NEXT DOOR TO PRIMARY SCHOOL.

'Fuck.' I let out; I couldn't hold it in.

'Shit,' Charley uncharacteristically added. 'You thinking what I'm thinking?'

I picked up the salt. 'Quick grab the bloody candles,' I said, as we jumped up and headed back through to the flat.

ACKNOWLEDGEMENTS

Firstly, we'd like to thank Anne Hamilton our editor, she took our ramblings and made them shine, repeatedly. Without her, we'd never have been noticed by Dark Edge Press.

We'd like to thank everyone at Dark Edge Press who made our dreams come true. We still have imposter syndrome, but they gave us the courage to wake up every day saying, 'I'm an author!' for real.

To our respective families, who put up with our temper tantrums and sour faces, as we wrote this novel separately and together, thank you all for your everlasting support.

We'd like to thank each other for being brave enough to start writing together, not letting the arguments last longer than a month and for not killing each other while trying to work out our very different writing processes. Side note, compromise is important (evil grin).

Most importantly, we'd like to thank you, the reader, for buying our book – it was written for you and we sincerely hope you enjoyed it.

Authors M. A. Russo are a sister collective, but you'd be forgiven for thinking they were one and the same. They both started their careers as nurses, with Marina gaining a Masters in Health Psychology and a Diploma in Clinical Hypnotherapy, and Anita as a University Nurse Lecturer with a PhD in Cancer Studies. These backgrounds fuel their writing.

Both are now commercial photographers by day and writers by night. They even have similar hobbies. They both love to run, hike, walk their dogs, grow their own veg and create spectacular vegan meals. Neither can sing well, a regret they both share, as do others around them.

Individually, Marina is passionate about lifelong learning, yoga, photographing nature and art. Anita loves shoemaking, screenwriting and composing songs on her guitar.

Love crime fiction as much as we do?

Sign up to our associates program to be first in line to receive Advance Review Copies of our books, and to win stationary and signed, dedicated editions of our titles during our monthly competitions. Further details on our website: www.darkedgepress.co.uk

Follow @darkedgepress on Facebook, Twitter, and Instagram to stay updated on our latest releases.

Printed in Great Britain
by Amazon